TRUE LOVE 101

Guide to discovering, creating, and sustaining true love

Nancy L. Davis, LMSW, LMFT

BALBOA
PRESS
A DIVISION OF HAY HOUSE

Library of Congress Control Number: 2012918405

Balboa Press books may be ordered through booksellers or by contacting:

Balboa Press
A Division of Hay House
1663 Liberty Drive
Bloomington, IN 47403
www.balboapress.com
1-(877) 407-4847

ISBN: 978-1-4525-5992-6 (sc)
ISBN: 978-1-4525-5994-0 (hc)
ISBN: 978-1-4525-5993-3 (e)

Because of the dynamic nature of the Internet, any web addresses or links contained in this book may have changed since publication and may no longer be valid. The views expressed in this work are solely those of the author and do not necessarily reflect the views of the publisher, and the publisher hereby disclaims any responsibility for them.

The author of this book does not dispense medical advice or prescribe the use of any technique as a form of treatment for physical, emotional, or medical problems without the advice of a physician, either directly or indirectly. The intent of the author is only to offer information of a general nature to help you in your quest for emotional and spiritual well-being. In the event you use any of the information in this book for yourself, which is your constitutional right, the author and the publisher assume no responsibility for your actions.

Any people depicted in stock imagery provided by Thinkstock are models, and such images are being used for illustrative purposes only.
Certain stock imagery © Thinkstock.

Printed in the United States of America

Balboa Press rev. date: 10/12/2012

CONTENTS

PREFACE

The intent of this book is to be a primer of the building blocks necessary to discover, create, and sustain a truly loving relationship with ourselves and our significant others. It is a distillation of the principles and practices that I have found to be most helpful not only in the lives of my clients, but in my life as well.

I still remember the first couple that I was assigned to help with their marital problems. I was twenty-five and single. They had been married for some time. When I asked what their concerns were, the wife began by saying, "I am very upset that he never talks, is always tired, and doesn't really seem to care about what I feel!" I clearly remember feeling that I really had no idea of where to go from there. The thought then occurred to me that I could at least do "active listening." So I said, "So you are upset that he never talks, is always tired, and doesn't seem to really care about what you feel." She replied, "No, that's not it at all!" At that point, all I remember is the panic I felt.

Since that time, I have learned a great deal. One of the things that I have learned is illustrated by this story. Most people do not really hear and understand the meaning of their own thoughts and feelings, let alone their spouses'. Many relationships are like the blind leading the blind. The journey begins with great hopes, fantasies, and expectations but no road map. Eventually, one-half to two-thirds of all relationships end in confusion, blaming, hurt, anger, and, ultimately, divorce or separation.

This book is meant to be a road map that provides what is necessary to discover, create, and sustain true love. The book is divided into four parts. The first part provides an understanding of the three basic stages of relationships. The second part discusses the importance of knowing who we are. It provides an explanation of our inherent guidance system, which is capable of providing us with all the necessary information we need to discover, create, and sustain true love. The third part clarifies our most basic needs and the power they have to control us, unless we consciously choose to respond to these needs. And finally, the last part explains the truly loving practices that are necessary for us to sustain true love.

I believe our most intimate relationships are potentially the greatest source of learning about true love. It is my fondest hope that all who read and do the "homework" in this book will ultimately know the joy of discovering, creating, and sustaining true love.

ACKNOWLEDGMENTS

I want to thank all of my clients who have shared their lives with me over the past thirty-five years. It has been such a privilege to know and care about you. I feel like words are inadequate to express what this journey has meant to me. Your lives are so precious, and it is my deepest hope that you are each continuing to know that truth.

The stories I have shared in this book are always a compilation of experiences. If they sound familiar, it is because we are not alone. There are always others who have shared the challenges and joys of healing. All names are fictitious.

For all the clients, friends, and family members who have encouraged me over the years to write down what I have shared with them, thank you.

I want to thank those who have most dearly loved me. Looking into the mirror of those relationships has provided great wisdom and healing.

I also want to thank all the people at Balboa Press for providing the guidance and skill necessary to publish this book.

And finally, I want to thank my precious love, Lynne. She is truly the best present I have ever received. Each day is a gift that I am so grateful to share.

CHAPTER ONE

The Journey to True Love

I deeply care about true love. I believe, within the journey of learning how to discover and sustain true love, exits the best hope we have individually or as a planet to survive and ultimately thrive. I also believe that where we are most motivated to value love is in relationship to ourselves, our spouse or significant other, and our children.

Most people want to have a partner/spouse/significant other. There are various names for this primary person in our lives, but no matter what the name, if that most intimate relationship is working well, we feel much more excited, hopeful, and energized by life. If that relationship is causing disappointment, fear, jealousy, or physical or emotional pain, we are miserable. It affects how we feel about every other area of our lives. We so want a successful relationship, and yet most people do not know how to create what they want. Statistics vary but suggest that from 50 to 60 percent of people fail at being able to sustain a successful relationship, and many of those still in a primary relationship do not seem to be happy.

1

We all enter a committed relationship assuming it will succeed. However, most of us have never really received the education or the tools needed to actually be successful. People have often turned to religion as a way to find answers to help their failing relationships. They have grown up being taught that "God is love," so they reason that religious teachers should be able to help them. Unfortunately, too many people have experienced judgment by these teachers, as well as inequality and lectures about the various rules to follow, rather than learning how to sustain true love.

Today, many people are more likely to turn to psychology and psychotherapists for help. The literal meaning of *psychology* is the "knowledge of spirit." Ironically, while many psychotherapists strive to teach people how to love themselves and each other, they would never mention the word *spirit*.

There are many therapeutic approaches that work with one or more aspects of healing. For example, cognitive therapy looks at how we think. By comparison, cognitive behavioral therapy looks at how we think and behave. Most approaches are helpful to some extent, but most ignore wholeness. Consequently, I often compare psychotherapy to the story of the blind men touching the elephant to find out what it is like. When they describe their experience to each other, each is very confident that he is describing the elephant, while in actuality, each is only describing one aspect of the elephant.

"Whole-I-ness" is ultimately what we all need to heal. One definition of *healing* is "to make whole." *Whole-I-ness* is not about being perfect or alone. It is about each person choosing to become more fully who he or she is. When each individual strives for wholeness, one plus one becomes more than two. If individuals value who they are, each person in the relationship will find that he or she is better off because of the relationship, rather than diminished. To be whole, we must reclaim that we are spiritual, mental, emotional, and physical beings. All of these aspects of self are communicating important information to us about how to discover and sustain true love with ourselves and others. If we are willing to honestly listen, amazing wisdom and guidance resides within each of us.

Knowing how to discover and sustain true love in relationships has only become more relevant in the United States over the past few decades. Historically, marriage as a legal contractual agreement kept most unions together. Women were not allowed to own property or work and therefore literally could not survive without a man.

The 1960s were the beginning of liberating men and women from contractual law that required them to stay together. For the first time, there was a massive shift in thinking about relationships. Women rose up as never before and began the fight for equality and control over their bodies, which continues to this day. Phrases like "battle of the sexes," "make love, not war," "love the one you're with," "male chauvinist pig," and "sexual harassment" began to transform our relationships. Underneath all this confusion and conflict, the desire for true love remained.

Not only do statistics tell us that our marriages are not lasting, but also, more recently, the census data tells us that, for the first time, less than 50 percent of people are even bothering to marry. More people than ever are questioning the validity of the marriage contract beyond that of a document that defines the legal rights for their relationship and their children. Clearly, legal documents no longer have the power to bind relationships.

This book is a guide to learning how to discover, create, and sustain true love. It is based on my experience over several decades as a psychotherapist working with individuals and couples. During that time, I had one primary focus, which was to find the clearest and most helpful approach to empower clients to create the successful relationships they desired.

I will be briefly discussing the first two stages of relationships where most people get stuck and never really progress farther, to the true love stage. I will then be focusing on the elements involved in being able to discover and progress to this final stage. Finally, I will explain the practices involved in sustaining a truly loving relationship.

There is a very wise saying, "To know and to not do, is to not yet know." Because of this necessity "to know and do" in order to experience what we desire, at the end of each knowledge section, I have assigned homework to encourage you to practice what you have learned. It is my utmost hope that you will choose to learn and apply the tools offered in this book so that you may know the joy of discovering, creating, and sustaining a truly loving relationship.

PART ONE

Three Stages of Relationships

Mastery Lesson:

Only through true love will our relationships thrive.

CHAPTER TWO

First Stage: Trust and Innocence

If we are honest about what initially draws us to another, no matter what our age, it is often simple and sweet: "He's cute," or "She's hot." If feelings are mutual, we will want to spend more time with that person. Depending on the strength of the attraction, it is amazing how quickly we can jump into a relationship. We call, we text, and we e-mail. We want to spend as much time as possible with that person. We think about the person. We dream about him or her. We imagine how our life with this individual will be. We get high on intimacy.

So many of us have come from families where we do not feel loved and connected. We do not feel safe emotionally and sometimes physically. We do not feel special, unique, important, adequate, or powerful enough to create what we need in life to thrive. These are such basic needs. Even if we don't think about them, these needs are ever present and driving our choices. When we meet someone we are attracted to who seems to care about us, we easily assume how wonderful this person is. We can't wait to be close to the person. We so want to be loved. We so want to feel safe. Now we have met someone whom we think/feel will be that person.

NANCY L. DAVIS, LMSW, LMFT

Sally and Jack met on the Internet and briefly dated from a distance. It seemed they were the people each had been searching for. Soon Jack moved from South Carolina to Michigan so they could be together. During their brief long-distance dating, they had never had a fight and were confident that their relationship would last. After Jack moved in with Sally, they discovered that Sally was very neat and Jack was not. Sally was working, and Jack was trying to find a job. These differences and others soon led to arguments and the threat that what once had felt like an ideal relationship would end in despair and disappointment.

In this first stage of relationships, we can be so innocent and can quickly give our trust away because we believe how we feel will never end. We are vulnerable to making decisions based on how we feel because of the stories we have told ourselves about this person rather than taking the time to create experiences that would tell us who this person really is.

In time, trust and innocence give way to something much more complex. Sooner or later, life gives us the opportunity to discover more about ourselves as well as who that other person is. Sometimes we are shocked at what we discover: "I can't believe you said that!" "I can't believe you would choose to behave that way. I can't believe you had an affair. "I can't believe I did not realize you were lying." "I can't believe I left South Carolina for you. What did I ever see in you?" "I can't believe how stupid I was to fall for your lies. I can't believe I trusted you." "What is wrong with you?" "What is wrong with me that I was attracted to you?"

Sometimes we give in to anger and try to make the other person change so that he or she matches what our trusting and innocent voice wants to be true. We tell the person, "You will never see that woman (or man) again!" "You have to start behaving differently if

8

you expect me to stay!" Or we try to strike bargains with ourselves: "He did not really mean that hurtful thing he said (or did)." "She won't do that again." "I know he (she) loves me. He was just going through a bad time."

These responses are all stages of loss. Anger, denial, depression, and bargaining are all the mental/emotional responses we come up with because we do not want to lose the feeling/belief that the person we were attracted to deserves our trust and innocence. Our inner child or deep longings talk to us about simply wanting to be loved and to be successful in creating our heart's desires.

Being loved and feeling safe and adequate to create what we long for are the most core needs we have. Every day our actions, attitudes, and attractions come from trying to get these needs fulfilled in some way. When we are not fully conscious of how these needs drive us, we innocently pick a partner/spouse and invest in that relationship, trusting our dreams will be fulfilled. All the ways that our parents have hurt, disappointed, and not fulfilled the desires, needs, and dreams we had as children (even if we don't remember what they were and believe we had a perfect childhood) have been taken into this relationship. We innocently trust that this person we love will heal, fulfill, and successfully create a "happily ever after" relationship with us. This experience happens so quickly and innocently that we usually have no idea what is going on until something happens and we start to feel some kind of emotional, physical, or mental pain.

Pain makes us question our assumptions. Pain makes us want to judge the other person or ourselves. Pain makes us want to give up the hope of having a successful relationship. Pain brings us to crossroads of choice. We can either give up all hope of having a successful relationship and take no responsibility for the relationship failing and blame the other person so we can start all over again in trust and innocence (once lost, it can never be felt in the same way). Or we can choose to become more aware of how to actually have a truly loving relationship. **Becoming more aware begins with questioning rather than judging. Why did that relationship not work out?**

There is much we can learn from this stage of relationship that can help move us toward being able to discover and sustain "true love" if we are willing. Here are some of the potential strengths and lessons from experiencing the relationship stage of **trust and innocence.**

Strengths

1. Being in touch with the feeling of an open, loving heart is where joy comes from.
2. Being in touch, with feeling attracted to someone, wakes us up to the possibility of true love.
3. Our innocence, infused with feeling loved and safe, wakes us up to our dreams of what life could be.

Wisdom Lessons

1. We need to experience at least "four seasons" with someone before we can begin to really know someone. The term "four seasons" is symbolic of the fact that it takes time to know someone. This process cannot be fast-forwarded. Trust and innocence must be balanced with strength and wisdom.

   We need the wisdom to know that trust takes time to earn. Words are not enough. We must observe actions long enough to see what is true. If words and actions are not the same, great pain, confusion, anger, sadness, and many forms of discontentment will follow. This discomfort is good because it tells us that something is very wrong. Just like when the fire alarm goes off. Pain is meant to get our attention so that we can take care of ourselves. We need the strength to see and act on what is true rather than cling to what we innocently want to believe and trust.

2. We must understand how we have been wounded. Do we question our lovability or adequacy? Without knowing ourselves, it is impossible to accurately see anyone else. This of course makes it very difficult to choose a relationship which can succeed.

3. This stage of relationship gives us the dream of what is possible. We must recognize how much of the relationship is the story or dream that we are hoping for versus a possible reality. Even when this kind of relationship ends, it is important to appreciate the dream of what we were hoping for. This dream is often our inspiration and hope that true love is possible. Our challenge is to figure out how to put a foundation under our desire for true love so it can actually become a reality.

During this first stage of relationship, we are not wise. We don't really understand how to discover and sustain true love. It just feels good and we go for it.

CHAPTER THREE

Second Stage: Building Hopes and Dreams

At some point along our journey of wanting to create a relationship, we will want to move away from the parents we grew up with. We will want to create our own home and primary relationship. For most of us, dating is a nightmare. We long for someone we can build a life with. All of the pain and drama of past relationships are collected as stories that we laugh or cry about with friends or just try to forget. When we meet that person that we fall in love with, hope is renewed. All of the dreams that we have been collecting are dusted off. We want to imagine, talk, plan, and start to move toward building a life together. If our hearts have been broken or we have just dated enough to feel rejection, we approach this new possibility of a relationship with some caution. We are no longer innocent. We don't immediately trust someone.

Chronologically, we are usually in our twenties or early thirties, but this may also happen when we are older. We may be in college, graduate school, or we may have been working for a while. We feel grown up and experienced. We've been in love, had sex, and feel very hopeful that we can create a life with someone. Often for men, a committed relationship or marriage represents the possibility of having sex on a regular basis without all the work that goes into finding someone. For women, they are usually thinking about the possibility of feeling loved, having children, and creating a family with someone.

During the dating process, each person usually has certain tests they are putting the other person through. How often and willing is she to have sex, and what kind of sex? How well does he dress? Do my friends like him? Is s/he fun? What kind of education/ job does s/he have? What are the spiritual/religious beliefs? How many kids does s/he want to have? Does he talk about his feelings? How attracted to him/her am I? Can we carry on a conversation? Etcetera. We all have our own tests. If the tests are passed well enough, people proceed with creating a life together.

We have probably all heard of the honeymoon period of a relationship. This is the period where all is sunshine and light. No one has bad breath, and if they do, it doesn't bother you. Annoying habits are still cute, and there is a layer of frosting on any possible irritant. We all also know that something happens, and at some point, conflicts start to arise. The honeymoon is officially over.

During this stage of the relationship, we have a lot of idealism about what it takes to have a successful relationship. But we also have some adult, mature thoughts about how we are going to be different from our parents. We are no longer just innocent. We are more aware of self-doubts and insecurities. We know that, even though the honeymoon is over, we want to stick with this relationship and make it work. Our hopes, dreams, and good will go a long way during this stage of relationship. Conflicts seemingly come and go and life goes on. The house and furniture are purchased. Routines of life are settled into. Children are born. The man cave is created.

In time, something seems to change. Couples stop easily moving through conflict. For some people, it seems to begin to really matter who is right and who is wrong in a particular argument. For some, it is very painful and maddening that advice is imposed rather than emotional support given. Conflicts seem to happen more often and feel worse, like a wound that is never really healing but keeps being reopened. The toll of unresolved differences, unmet needs, sleeplessness, financial struggles, the exhaustion of arguments and unsuccessful compromises, etc. all become the forces that are threatening the fundamental ability to feel loved and secure in this primary relationship. Couples become confused, scared, angry, sad, and threatened. They don't know exactly how they got to this point, and they don't know exactly how to fix what is threatening the survival of their relationship.

During this stage of relationship, because we have the commitment and ideals of wanting a successful relationship, we usually are not in touch with realizing that we really don't know how to create what we want. It's almost as if, because we want it and because we assume we know how to have a successful relationship, we assume that we will have one. Unfortunately, wanting, assuming, and expecting are not the same as really knowing what it takes to create something. Consequently, we are often expecting something from the other person that we may or may not have been aware of or even asked for. Nevertheless, we are really hurt, angry, devastated, and/or confused. Sometimes we can feel very confident that if the other person would just do, change, or say whatever I think or feel the person should be doing, changing, or saying, then everything would be fine. (This strategy never works.)

If we move into minimizing, denying, ignoring, repressing, rationalizing, blaming, judging, arguing, or any other kind of choice where we do not figure out what needs to change, the relationship will turn into a pressure cooker. Gradually over enough time, tension, judgment, resentment, and stories about the other person will continue to collect until one day the spaghetti sauce hits the ceiling. The relationship blows up.

Sometimes we notice we just don't feel that attracted to that person anymore, we feel chronically sad, or we feel tired and irritable a lot. Or we feel like the other person can't do anything right. The interactions seem to be more like negotiations about the functional things that have to be taken care of and much less about the fun of creating and sharing experiences together.

Sometimes the ending of the relationship comes in the form of an announcement. We have probably all heard of situations where one spouse, seemingly out of nowhere, makes the announcement that s/he wants a divorce. Or decides to have an affair. Often those choices go together because, over time, our hopes and dreams have faded. We have gradually been disconnecting from the relationship one unresolved feeling or one judgmental thought at a time. Until finally judgment, resentment, and disappointment have taken the place of love, patience, and passion.

When we meet someone, where suddenly hopes and dreams of having a loving sexy relationship are renewed, often it is very tempting to just start over, believing things will be different with this new person. In reality, this stage will just be recycled again unless different choices are made. Or we may just give up on having a loving relationship.

Some research has shown that many middle-aged women would rather not remarry. They want to have a companion to have sex with and do activities with, but they want to go home to peace and quiet. Past relationships have spent their trust and innocence as well as their hopes and dreams of a loving and safe relationship. One-half to two-thirds of all relationships are ending in divorce or separation. Can you blame anyone for giving up on or being skeptical of having and sustaining a truly loving relationship?

However, sometimes during this stage of relationship, we may remind ourselves that we knew s/he wasn't perfect and we choose to be hopeful that whatever conflicts or differences there are can be resolved. We recognize that we are different from each other. We recognize the need to learn how to move through conflict so that we can understand ourselves and the other person better. We choose to step back from the pain, shame, and anger. We choose to stop blaming the other person and start learning about what we are each doing to destroy the joy and well-being of our relationship.

When we find the strength and wisdom to stop blaming and start opening to the possibility of learning how to create a very different truly loving relationship, we move on to the next stage of relationships. Here are some of the strengths and wisdom lessons from the "hopes and dreams" stage of relationships.

Strengths

1. Leaving home and noticing that there are different kinds of people and relationships is the beginning of having a broader awareness of what might be possible.
2. Wanting a primary relationship encourages us to move on in life and try to actively create our ideal.
3. It is the beginning of noticing that an adult, interdependent relationship could really enhance life.

Wisdom Lessons

1. During this stage of relationship, we all want to believe we know how to succeed at creating a loving, lasting relationship, even though we have never been taught how to accomplish this.
2. Without guidance, we will most likely recreate life as we knew it as a child. No matter how much we want it to be different.
3. Conflict is never the problem. It is what we do with conflict that will determine the success or failure of our relationships. Conflict, just like physical pain, can draw our attention to what needs to be healed. This awareness of pain or discomfort awakens us to the need for change. This is a major crossroad for most relationships.

The majority of relationships in the United States end at this stage of relationship. Fortunately, the best is yet to come for those who choose not to give up on their deep desire to discover and sustain true love.

CHAPTER FOUR

Third Stage: True Love

This is the stage that, inherently, we all long for, even if we don't know what to call it or how to get there. There is something in all of us, at such a visceral level, that knows when we feel loved and safe. When I use the word *safe*, I do mean physically safe, but I also mean spiritually, mentally, and emotionally safe. To know that we are safe to express our inspiration, creative ideas, thoughts, and feelings versus being shamed, judged, and intimidated is fundamental to sustaining a truly loving relationship.

There are several challenges to being able to discover and sustain a truly loving relationship. One challenge is the word itself. For our deepest, most intimate emotional expression, we say, "I love you." But we also say, "I love hot dogs!" Clearly, it is important to figure out what that word means, and are we both meaning the same thing when we say it?

A second challenge is that our music, movies, romance novels, etc. have become our reference points of understanding what love is. Unfortunately, in many songs, it is associated with, "I'll die without you. I can't live without you." In movies and romance novels, we are taught that being with the most handsome man who has a fast car and lots of money, and the most beautiful woman with long blonde hair and the body of a sixteen-year-old model, is where true love resides.

A third challenge is that the imbedded beliefs about relationships, which we unconsciously store away in our belief box, come from whatever experiences we've had from living with our parents. From these early experiences, we collect the internal feelings and beliefs of our five-year-old, twelve-year-old, sixteen-year-old, etc. as to what the other person should say, do, be, give, sound like, etc. if the person really loved us.

The last challenge I will mention is most of us, including our parents, have never taken classes on such topics as discovering and sustaining a loving relationship, creating and sustaining sexual intimacy, and understanding how to make relationships stronger through conflict resolution. Therefore, most of us enter a primary committed relationship with unrealistic expectations, many unmet needs, and no skill set or understanding of what is involved with discovering, creating, and sustaining a truly loving relationship.

Even with these apparent obstacles, most of us long for a truly loving relationship. Research tells us that people are happier, better off financially, and live longer when their relationship is an enjoyable one. While we have these challenges to overcome, we have it in us to discover and sustain true love.

It has been my privilege to work with incredibly successful, doctors, corporate executives, lawyers, educators, architects, scientists, writers, carpenters, pipe fitters, realtors, artists, etc. These clients have been amazingly talented people. Yet they would go home and feel inadequate and unloved. They may have been responsible for a multimillion budget, saving someone's life, or designing a building during their work hours, but one look or comment from their spouse could make them feel utterly inadequate or unloved in less than five minutes. These are all powerful people and yet they too had to learn how to sustain a loving connection. They had to choose to stop using their power to try to win power struggles in order to be "right." Rather, they had to choose to learn how to sustain what they really wanted, a loving, sexy, successful relationship.

The reality is that most of us need help to ever experience this stage of relationship. Somehow, we have to figure out how to put a foundation under the trusting and innocent dreams and longings we had as a child to be loved and safe. We have to pick ourselves up from the disappointment of failing at creating our hopes and dreams of a successful, lasting relationship. We need to reclaim the word *love* from the hot dog stand and all the air brushing and fantasies of Hollywood.

The good news is that if you are reading this, you still have hope and desire and you have found someone who really can teach you how to experience the true-love stage of relationship.

When people make the choice to create such a relationship, they realize the effort involved with discovering and sustaining a truly loving relationship is actually simpler and infinitely more gratifying than all the struggles they were having. The rest of this book will teach how to discover, create, and sustain truly loving relationships.

PART TWO

Foundation of True Love

Mastery Lesson:

We must know who we are in order to discover true love.

CHAPTER FIVE

The Importance of Knowing Who We Are

Whether we are building an airplane, creating a painting, or creating a successful relationship, nothing meaningful is created without knowledge and the practice of applying this awareness. We cannot just read a book about golf and expect to walk on the greens and immediately be able to play golf. We need to learn about the sport and the equipment. The various elements of the game are broken down and practiced over and over again. Eventually, the understanding and practice become integrated and we can say that we enjoy the experience of playing golf. We know playing golf can be very frustrating, but when we are successful, it is very gratifying. One of my favorite T-shirts says, "I hate golf. I hate golf. I hate golf. Good shot. I love golf. I love golf. I love golf." Truly, there is something deeply satisfying about putting a small ball in a small hole a long way away.

Succeeding in a truly loving relationship is metaphorically similar to this process. In golf as well as other aspects of life, education leads to understanding. Understanding leads to the ability to make different choices. Practicing making different choices can lead to the experience of discovering, creating, and sustaining a loving, safe, successful relationship, one choice/step at a time. Our education needs to start with a framework of understanding, which can help us work with the guidance that resides within us.

We are complex and magnificent beings beyond the comprehension of doctors, scientists, or religious teachers. We are still evolving in our understanding of the complexity of who we are. We often take ourselves for granted and mostly don't even think about who we are. Yet there are complex processes occurring which are shaping and informing every interaction and outcome we experience. A very simple analogy is the complexity of the inner workings of a computer. Most of us do not fully comprehend all of the complexity involved in this amazing piece of equipment. However, if we learn enough about the amazing capability and how to utilize it, we can really enhance our lives.

So even though we cannot fully comprehend our own amazing complexity, for the purposes of learning how to discover, create, and sustain true love, I would suggest that it is very helpful to be aware of what I am calling our five primary aspects. (These aspects are not meant to be concrete. Rather they are descriptions of experiential phenomena that most people can relate to.) They include the spiritual, mental, emotional, physical, and observing aspects of our being. Each of these aspects provides very important and personally unique information and guidance about how to discover, create, and sustain a truly loving relationship with ourselves and others.

Our spiritual, mental, emotional, and physical aspects are constantly giving us information. While the observing aspect has the ability to monitor, translate, and decide what choices we are going to make based on all the information we are receiving, our choices then bring us closer to or farther away from true love.

These aspects of self are like a built-in GPS. We often hear that information is power. I would say that the choices we make, based on this information, determine whether or not we are utilizing our power to create or destroy a truly loving relationship. We have the innate ability to discover and sustain a truly loving relationship by listening, understanding, and responding to the guidance or information we are receiving. Step-by-step, choice-by-choice, our observing self can guide us to the destination of a truly loving relationship.

One of the challenges we all have, however, is that we can easily use the "connectivity" technology we have to disconnect from ourselves as well as our relationships. Any external focus can easily distract us and leave us extremely vulnerable to not utilizing our internal guidance or our creative capability.

I am reminded of a friend who was directionally challenged so she purchased a GPS for her car. She then proceeded to not listen to it. Frequently, on trips I would hear her say to the GPS, "I don't want to turn there." The GPS would then talk back, saying, "Recalculating, recalculating, recalculating!" We are constantly receiving guidance from our various aspects about how to discover and sustain love. We, however, have to make the choice to listen and respond.

Each aspect of self also represents a way that we can connect with someone else. There are many patterns of connection. For example, some people may share a research interest and be very connected mentally. Some people go to bars to find someone to just connect with physically. Others may be very good friends and connect spiritually, mentally, and emotionally. However, when people come together and choose to draw on the wisdom of their "observing self" to lovingly connect spiritually, mentally, emotionally, and physically, they are able to discover, create, and sustain a deeply loving relationship.

I often compare these levels of connection to a piece of strong cloth. It is very difficult to pull a piece of fabric apart. But if there is a very small cut in the fabric, with enough pressure the cloth tears apart. In a primary relationship, if all these potential aspects of connections are present, it is very difficult to pull that relationship apart. However, if we are disconnecting from ourselves or each other spiritually, mentally, emotionally, or physically, each form of disconnection is like a cut in the cloth. Each form of disconnection adds to the vulnerability of that relationship splitting apart. Most people have disconnected from their relationship spiritually, mentally, and/or emotionally long before they ever finally leave physically. That is why it is very important to understand the significance of each of these aspects of self and how we can choose to utilize them to discover, create, and sustain true love.

CHAPTER SIX

Spiritual Aspect

The Greek translation of *psychology* is "the study of spirit, soul, breath, or life force." Unfortunately, the misuse of religion has made many of us want to ignore or disown the spiritual aspect of who we are. Recognizing the spiritual aspect of life is extremely important in creating our relationships. Our spiritual aspect has to do with recognizing what inspires us. Inspiration may occur through nature, music, religion, art, spirituality, children, pets, intuition, being of service, illness, death, etc. Being in spirit or inspired breathes life and meaning into our relationships. Inspiration, when listened to, guides us toward enjoyment, meaningful work, joy, renewed energy, passion, success, hope, trust, strength, compassion, peace, beauty, artistic expression, healing, and, ultimately, true love.

Falling in love seems to be one of the most common ways to experience inspiration. Seemingly out of nowhere, we are inspired to be giving, kind, creative, and attentive. Through the "eyes of love," we feel like we wake up and experience the kind of joy, hope, and desire we have only read about. All of a sudden, we are infused with energy and want to be the best we can be. We feel that anything might be possible.

Falling in love with someone is not something we can *think* our way into. It is not something we can force upon ourselves or anyone else. It is a gift that seems to just come to us. It is a transformative feeling or force which seems to exist in some unknown compartment within us. Seemingly out of nowhere, one day we can wake up and "discover" love.

As one of my clients, who happened to be an accountant, said, "I can add up all the pros and cons, and even if the con list is longer, there is something that draws me to this person. I just love her!" Love is the best present that exists within us all.

But as many of us who have received or given this gift of love know, it does not come with a lifetime guarantee. Our challenge is to take the inspiration and desire, which we have discovered from falling in love, and make the conscious choice to learn how to understand, nurture, strengthen, and ultimately sustain the experience of love.

There is much in life that we seem to be able to control, and there is also much that we cannot control. This continuum of controllable versus the uncontrollable is where we also have an opportunity to notice the spiritual aspect of ourselves. The more we try to control what is not controllable, the more anxious, angry, bitter, resentful, and out of control we can become. Let's face it. There is a part of all of us that probably thinks that if we could just control everything, everyone would be better off. We all know, however, that that is not reality. When we face experiences that are painful, confusing, and devastating, we are at a crossroad. All of my clients who are in recovery from any kind of addiction have learned that once they were able to turn the uncontrollable over to a "higher power," life began again for them.

Most people in our country believe that there is a force beyond them. For those who are open to this great dimension, which has been known by many names, there is the possibility of discovering and sharing the inspiration they have received while experiencing these "uncontrollable" spaces in life. It has been during the most painful times in my life that I have received the greatest clarity and inspiration to go on to create the greatest love of my life. Many people tell stories of their dark nights of the soul. They go on to describe how this experience transformed their lives completely.

One way to discover the spiritual aspect of self is to engage in self-reflection. Self-reflection is simply the ability to listen to our own intuitive truth about what energizes and inspires us. We need to listen and step-by-step create the kind of life experiences which are a reflection of loving ourselves and others. Without this awareness, life can feel like one long to-do list. We can function well and get stuff done, but it has no meaning. If we do not know and therefore cannot articulate what inspires us, it is not like that need just goes away.

If we minimize the importance of this aspect or any of the other aspects of ourselves, it is most likely that it is only a matter of time until something will get acted out. This is often the source of a midlife crisis. We may have received some kind of intuitive inspirational guidance about what work we needed to pursue when we were younger and talked ourselves out of it. At some point, we may not be able to live with the choices we have made and feel compelled to change. This can create a crisis and an opportunity.

Barb and Gerry went to graduate school together and were married soon after. They both entered the world of finance and quickly established a very busy opulent lifestyle. Several years into their relationship, Gerry got into a car accident. He was seriously injured, and he almost killed a pedestrian. He knew his judgment was impaired because, as usual, he had been drinking at the end of the day. This incident was a turning point for him. While recovering from his injuries, he realized that he was not happy. His father was an alcoholic, and he knew he had to face that he also had been abusing alcohol. He knew something had to change. In time, he knew he had to create work for himself that he could enjoy and find meaningful.

With his background in finance, he decided he would much rather work for a nonprofit organization, which did work that he believed in. At first, this was a very difficult adjustment for Barb. She even contemplated leaving him. In time, she realized how much more enjoyable their relationship was because their whole lives were not just focused on work. She actually enjoyed volunteering some of her time for the nonprofit. Together, they found experiences through volunteering, new friendships, and a lifestyle that fostered a loving relationship between them.

If we do not know, listen to, or discuss the importance of what inspires us, it not only means that we do not fully know ourselves, it also means that we have entered into a relationship where the other person cannot really know us either. This is one way that there can be a cut or disconnect in the fiber of what holds us together.

Homework: Share the spiritual aspect of who you are.

1. Write down your experiences, practices, and beliefs which inspire and energize you.
2. Share these with your significant other and discuss which are the most meaningful and enjoyable to you.
3. Consider how this awareness could affect the choices you make around work, play, and the kind of relationship you want to create.

CHAPTER SEVEN

Mental Aspect

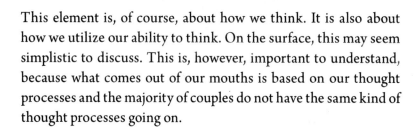

This element is, of course, about how we think. It is also about how we utilize our ability to think. On the surface, this may seem simplistic to discuss. This is, however, important to understand, because what comes out of our mouths is based on our thought processes and the majority of couples do not have the same kind of thought processes going on.

Our different thoughts portray our differences literally and symbolically. It is in this mental aspect where relationships begin to unravel. It seems to be such a knee-jerk reaction for most of us to judge what is different. Each judgmental thought collects to create a story. If we self-righteously hang onto our own way of thinking in order to rationalize, defend, debate, block, shame, blame, minimize, intimidate, overwhelm, and therefore prove we are "right," we will be creating disconnection and destroying any possibility for true love to be experienced. If, however, we use our differences to expand our experience of how to see and experience life, the resulting compassion and connection will continue our discovery of true love. Therefore, the willingness to listen and appreciate what the other person is actually communicating is an extremely important and ongoing challenge for most couples.

The reality is that most men and women do not access their brains or mental processes in the same way. Because men typically go to the left side of their brains when they are "thinking," they have more of a tendency to make statements, offer advice, draw conclusions (which can feel like pronouncements) rather than wanting to discuss things in great detail. The male brain does not typically access the feeling part of the brain when males are problem solving.

Whereas women typically access both the rational and emotional aspects of "thinking" (left and right sides of the brain). Whenever something is being discussed, it is understandable why most women are likely to utilize more words. Most women are literally accessing more of their brains when they are thinking. It is my understanding from learning about the neurobiology of girls and boys that 80 percent of male brains and 20 percent of female brains operate similarly. Just as 80 percent of female brains and 20 percent of male brains operate similarly. You can probably see why this difference alone has affected so many couples.

It is such a stereotype that women want to talk more than men. Women want to know what their male partners are feeling. Women often take it for granted that men could easily discuss their feelings if they wanted to. Men have typically felt irritated with what they consider to be long discussions about paint colors, where to go for dinner, which dress looks better, and any delving into wanting to know what they are feeling about almost anything. The reality is the emotional part of most male brains takes effort to access. If expressing feelings was not encouraged when they were younger, it is something they may never be very good at. Often men can only easily access what I call big emotions like anger. I will also add that the same-sex couples I work with may or may not have their brains processing information and experiences in the same way as well.

The typical male brain hears what most women are saying as feelings, description, or details (translation: *"blah, blah, blah,* still waiting to hear a behavioral description of what she is wanting me to do"*) or more description ("now he is lost," agitated, spacing out). Suddenly she stops talking and says, "So how do you feel about that?" This is when the *deer in the headlights* feeling can happen for many men. At this point, they have a choice. They can talk about themselves and how they don't really care or have any feelings about what she was just talking about (that doesn't feel safe) so they usually don't answer the question. Instead, they offer some kind of advice. At that point, at least inside, they feel adequate because what they said seemed rational to them. But of course, the woman feels irritated because he did not share his feelings. Additionally, she lets him know that she does not need to be told what to do. This communication process leaves her feeling unloved and him feeling inadequate.

Most couples do not really understand how their brains are working differently. Consequently, it has been very difficult for couples to have realistic, compassionate expectations of the communication process. Too often discussions are more like debates about who is right and who is wrong. These "power struggles," as I call them, are extremely common and eventually erode the connection between people.

How we discuss anything is basic to how loved a person feels and how much sex there is going to be in a relationship. If we feel heard and understood, we feel connected with and valued. Therefore, how we talk to each other and respond to each other determines how well we can discover and sustain what is important to us individually and together. **How to communicate, based on a compassionate understanding of differences is a skill that must be learned and practiced.**

A very quick assessment of how your brain functions can be made by answering the following questions honestly.

1. Do you enjoy hearing about or discussing feelings?
2. Do you really enjoy discussing what color would look better in a room?
3. Do you have a tendency to make statements rather than ask questions?
4. If you are listening to your spouse or partner, are you waiting to hear what she or he wants you to do?

Obviously, if you answer yes to the first two questions, you are more likely to be accessing your emotional and rational sides of the brain. If you answered yes to the last two questions, you are more likely to be accessing your rational brain most often.

Now that you are aware of these basic differences, you might be able to appreciate that people need to learn how to communicate in order to be heard and understood. Once we can communicate with understanding, realistic expectations, and compassion, we feel more adequate to create the connection we want.

Homework: Learn how to create connection through communication.

Tips for Most Women

1. Start with listening to yourself and understanding what it is you really want or need. Write it down. Ask, "Is this really mine to take care of?" If not, go to number two.
2. Be clear on what results you are looking for and let your spouse know, upfront, what you are wanting. For example, are you just wanting to be listened to, or are you wanting some kind of response? If it is a response, is it verbal, behavioral, or emotional? Communication is not meant to be a guessing game. The more clearly you can articulate what you are asking for, the more likely your spouse will be able to succeed at meeting your request.
3. Where appropriate, provide a clear time line. Example: "Would you be able to do that before dinner?"

Tips for Most Men

1. Accept that your life will be easier if you just admit that you are not clear on what is being expected of you and ask for clarification.
2. Remember that communication is about connection and understanding each other better. Having a discussion is not a sporting event where there is a winner and a loser. You do not have to be right or have all the answers in order to be a very adequate, successful husband or partner.

3. Respond with a question rather than an answer/ statement. For example, "How can I be helpful?" "Can you tell me why you are upset?"

Tips for Both

1. Learn and practice effective listening. You will find a guide for this in the sustaining practices chapter. Most often, people are responding to what they thought they heard rather than what the speaker actually said. Effective listening ensures that we accurately hear what is said, we understand the meaning of what is said, and we are, therefore, responding to what the person really is saying and meaning.
2. Power struggles about what the other person really said or meant are never sexy. Stay open. Just because you *thought* you heard what was said, it does not mean you accurately interpreted what was being shared. Let the other person clarify rather than staying attached to your interpretation.

CHAPTER EIGHT

Emotional Aspect

Regarding how we think, we have already been discussing that there is an aspect of the brain that generates feelings or emotions. Feelings, as I mentioned, can be more difficult for some people to access than others, but we all have them. Historically, feelings have been minimized, considered a weakness, and associated with women. From a young age, little boys have often been encouraged to not cry. In some religious/spiritual teachings, they have been associated with impulses and something to ignore. Consequently, many people experience a lot of confusion about what they feel.

Our feelings help us differentiate the uniqueness of who we are and they help us distinguish what is important to us. When we are able to know what we are feeling, why we are feeling that way, and what if anything needs to be done about what we are feeling, we are then able to utilize the information we are receiving emotionally to help us create and sustain true love.

Unfortunately, there are many strategies that people use to get rid of their feelings rather than value them as important guidance. However, whatever we disown owns us, even if we are not aware of it. Therefore, it is important to highlight some of the strategies people use to get rid of their feelings.

Strategies to Disown Feelings

One strategy would be the **hot potato strategy**. As soon as something uncomfortable is felt, most people seem to have a tendency to do whatever it takes to quickly get rid of it. Some people use drugs, alcohol, sex, food, gambling, gaming, shopping, sugar, watching TV, Facebook, etc. in order to stop or get rid of the feelings that are uncomfortable.

A second strategy can be the **remote control strategy**. This strategy is about believing if the external person/picture were to change, we would feel better. So we try to remotely control the other person in order to get him or her to do what we think would make us feel better.

A third strategy is to be "**Judge Judy**" and decide which feelings are "good" or "bad" therefore justifying ignoring, repressing, denying, etc. any "bad" feeling. Some feelings are obviously uncomfortable to have, but it is essential to understand that all feelings are giving us some kind of important information.

How we respond to discomfort is one of the most important decisions we will ever make. In discomfort lies some of the most relevant information we will ever receive about how to discover and sustain a truly loving relationship.

If I were to stick my hand on a hot stove, I really hope it hurts. This pain causes me to react quickly so that I don't do any more damage. At a physical level, we take this information for granted and immediately react to take care of our safety. When we feel bad in our relationships, it is actually letting us know that something hurtful is going on and needs to change. Once we understand this, we will eventually be grateful for the guidance of discomfort.

Without pain, most people would never wake up. Pain causes many of us to start questioning how life could be different. This questioning can be the beginning of trying to discover how to sustain a loving, safe relationship with ourselves and our significant others. Unfortunately, if we are not careful, our minds will quickly jump in and try to explain, blame, shame, deny, minimize, justify, etc. to quickly get rid of the pain. When this occurs, we have lost an opportunity to begin to understand that doing the opposite of what is causing us pain can take us a step closer to discovering how to create a truly loving, safe relationship.

Strategies to Misuse Feelings

Sometimes people are willing to have their feelings, but they misuse them. It is therefore also important to understand how some people misuse their feelings.

The first strategy to misuse feelings is the out-of-control **fire-hose approach**. The feelings are just sprayed all over the place. The reaction by others to this approach usually is rejection, avoidance, confusion, etc. Just like a fire hose is meant to be directed in a helpful way, our feelings are meant to help us not hurt ourselves or others. When they are used in a hurtful way, we will usually get a negative response back. This obviously does not help us create a loving, safe relationship.

The second misuse of feelings is the "**hang onto it for dear life**" approach. "Because you said/did/looked that way, I get to make a pronouncement about you, and it is the truth! Why do I know it's true? Because I *feeeeeel* this way!"

Using our feelings to make pronouncements about someone's intentions, thoughts, meaning, feelings, etc. usually leaves the other person feeling insignificant, angry, depressed, and/or out of control. We get into trouble when we feel like something is true and therefore become unwilling to consider what the other person's intention really is. This leads to debating and arguing rather than staying open to an opportunity for understanding and connection.

The third misuse of feelings is "**staying lost in the dark forest of feelings.**" Talking or thinking about our feelings over and over again without being open to finding the meaning can cause us to go around and around and get lost. Some people have lost who they are and what they are capable of. Instead, they have taken on their feelings as their identity. "I'm depressed. Who are you?" We do not want to get lost in the dark forest of feelings where we cannot see our feelings as arrows pointing us in a new direction of healing.

The Importance of Feelings

When listened to and understood, feelings are an extremely important source of information.

First of all, our feelings can **detect when the pain of disconnection is beginning** so that we can quickly repair the disconnection before it grows into feeling unloved or unsafe. Disconnecting from someone we are working to create a relationship with can happen in a split second. Without a way of detecting that something just happened that is potentially hurtful to the well-being of our relationship, we would function like robots. Experiences and information we learned growing up would be programmed or taken into our memory banks and we would continue to just function accordingly.

Through repeated experiences, we are programmed to recreate what seems normal, even if it feels bad. If we cannot work with and translate the guidance of our feelings, there is no hope for change to occur. We would just keep behaving in ways that are destructive to the well-being of our relationship. We would either not be aware or we would just keep defending our behavior until the relationship falls apart.

Secondly, our feelings **guide us to what I call our dark side**. Our dark side is where all that we don't want to acknowledge about ourselves resides. Without facing these thoughts, feelings, and beliefs, they will continue to hold power over us and we will never fully know our potential. We will also never fully know our partner/ spouse if we do not know their dark side as well. Turning on the light, facing what resides there, liberates us to truly know what love looks like, feels like, and acts like. We can never truly feel loved if we are hiding and avoiding that which makes us feel unlovable.

Finally, the **wisdom of responding to what we feel** by moving away from that which is abusive, demeaning, debilitating, etc. and toward that which is encouraging, hopeful, happy, exciting, strengthening, etc. is how we rightly use our power to sustain that which is true love.

Here is an example which illustrates many of the dynamics I just described:

Sandy would often try to have a conversation with Bill when he first got home from work. (Fire hose.) The response she got would often get, sounded like anger rather than interest. (Rejection.) She would respond to this by getting upset and telling him that obviously he was not interested in her day. (Judge Judy.) He would then respond, with more anger because that was not at all how he felt. (Remote Control.) Sandy would then build a case for why her feelings were obviously correct because of his tone, not making eye contact with her or not asking her any questions. (Hang onto it for dear life.) Bill would then respond by getting even angrier because he was tired of feeling like he could not do anything right. (More remote control.)

This is a common example of what happens in many relationships. Growing up, Sandy was neglected and did not feel loved by her parents. No one showed much interest in her life. Yet her father was quick to anger if he felt like she had done something wrong. Sandy was a very successful woman and had worked very hard to prove her worthiness. Yet she had buried the belief that she wasn't lovable in the shadows of her dark side. Every day it came out in some way. She was quick to judge Bill's anger as unloving.

With some guidance, Bill was able to give her reassurances that he really did love her and was interested in her day. He also explained that he was too tired, when he first got home, to have a conversation. This information was helpful, but Sandy had to really ponder letting go of her belief about not being lovable. She had to own what was in her dark side. She had to stop blaming Bill for making her feel unlovable and own her self-doubt about being loveable as well as her doubt about any man being able to love. Rationally, she knew that Bill really did care about her. Unfortunately, the cycle of behaviors that they both participated in over and over again resulted in her feeling unlovable, just as she did when she was growing up.

Eventually with guidance, Sandy was able to stop being judgmental and unloving toward her husband and herself. She stopped setting up scenarios where she would not feel loved and he would feel inadequate. She started to take in his love and acknowledge that she was loveable. She began asking if it was a good time to talk. When he was able to give her attention, he would say yes, and they would have an enjoyable conversation. He got to feel successful and adequate to meet her needs, and she got to feel loved and cared about. Through therapy, he also understood his anger better and was able to speak up sooner if he was unavailable.

I know it may seem like an obvious solution for her to just talk to him at a different time, but this is how powerful our buried beliefs can be. I often say to people that feelings do not have to be logical. In fact, they can seem more like a clue or riddle that is directing us toward the important treasure of understanding what beliefs and wounds are driving us. Without this understanding of what are we feeling and why, we do not have the awareness we need to create a different life experience.

Feelings educate us about the uniqueness of who we are. Feelings guide us to a much deeper understanding of what it means to love ourselves and others. **We must choose to stop avoiding or misusing our feelings and accept the challenge to discover and value the information they are communicating to us.**

Homework: Learn to stop the cycle of avoidance and misuse by translating the wisdom of feelings.

1. We need to ask, "What am I feeling? Why am I feeling that way? What, if anything, do I need to do in response to these feelings?" The answers to these questions

guide, liberate, and empower us to create the true love we are longing for.

2. Write down the answers to these questions as a practice of really listening and responding. Without hearing, understanding, and responding to our own feelings, it is very unlikely that anyone else will be successful at this endeavor either.

3. If you are someone who feels mostly one emotion like anger, it can actually be helpful to just ask, "What else might I be feeling?" There is some part of us that knows and may just answer our question, because we have paused long enough to consider what else we might be feeling. It is also helpful to consider a list of feeling words like, mad, glad, scared, frustrated, helpless, overwhelmed, impatient, etc. and notice which one seems to feel right for the situation at hand. Now go back up to the first homework in this section and continue asking the rest of the questions about your emotional guidance. Discovering more of who we are allows us to more fully experience true love.

CHAPTER NINE

Physical Aspect

The physical aspect of who we are is the only aspect of self we can actually see. Our bodies are like billboards. They perpetually are communicating something to us. Our sexual response tells us if we are attracted to someone. Our faces show a myriad of emotions. Our weight can tell us if we are misusing our body. Our bodies can also reflect what is going on with the other aspects of who we are spiritually, mentally, and emotionally. If we are unaware of something we are thinking, feeling, or doing which is not loving, it will ultimately show up in our bodies. The billboard of our bodies communicates many messages for those who are able to read or translate them.

We need to understand what our bodies need in terms of food, exercise, rest, sex, comfort, and sometimes medication. To take care of these needs is an active way of truly loving our body and appreciating the importance of it. Too often, the body is taken for granted or misused in some way. If we want to enjoy a loving relationship with someone else, we must have that with our own body.

Our need for sexual intimacy is very important to be aware of. Often for men, the desire to have sex leads to feeling closer to their spouse. For women, often there is the desire for closeness, before there is a willingness to have sex. We also know most men, because of the higher levels of testosterone, may be thinking about sex as often as every six minutes. (The amount of time varies, but we know it is frequent.) Most women have no idea what that might feel like unless they have taken testosterone.

It is very important that men not expect women to initiate sex as often as they would. Most women will never have that level of testosterone. It is also important for women to stop thinking it is bad that "he can't just cuddle. He always wants to have sex!" The fact that he is attracted to you is a good thing, and if you are clear and ask to cuddle, men are very capable of that kind of closeness.

I often remind my clients that they did not choose a clone, and if they had, it would be boring. Sexual intimacy is essential in order to maintain and strengthen the bond between people. We do not want to turn the innate differences between us into a power struggle. We must find compassion in understanding our differences, appreciate the gifts of these differences, and negotiate the compromises which sustain sexual connection. Without it, it is usually just a matter of time until the fabric of the relationship is torn apart by someone acting out sexually.

We know there are infinite ways to act out with our bodies and show externally what unmet needs and wounds we are carrying around internally. We also know that there are infinite ways that we can use the power which lies within our bodies to create a loving expression. It is this ability to use our bodies as vehicles to create and express love that we all long for. We all know that words without actions are meaningless. We also know that actions without love are ultimately meaningless as well. When we empower our bodies to take action on the wisdom and guidance we have received spiritually, mentally, and emotionally, we can delight in our choice to discover and sustain true love.

Homework: Learn to value the wisdom of your body.

1. List the health concerns that you have and what needs to be done to take care of your body. Decide how you are going to take action to respond to these concerns.
2. Discuss the importance of sexual intimacy. Describe the kind of sexual intimacy that makes you feel more loved and excited to be with your spouse. Plan to have sexual intimacy. Do not wait for it to happen "naturally." As we age, you could be waiting a very long time. During this time, the strength of your unique, intimate connection is waning.
3. Feed your body in a loving way and exercise regularly.

CHAPTER TEN

Observing Aspect

We are complex beings. We are constantly being given information from our inspiration, thoughts, and feelings, as well as our bodily guidance. If we were just flooded with data, we would freeze up and no one would leave the house. Fortunately, most people have the ability to observe all this information. Being aware allows us to listen, translate meaning, and decide the best course of action to create a truly loving, safe relationship. Our observing self tells us the difference between what is potentially impulsive, reactionary, rejecting, and hurtful versus meaningful, thoughtful, loving, and helpful, before we choose to act. This is our grand central station. If we make loving choices, our relationship stays on track. If we don't, we have clashes and collisions, which can dismantle our relationship.

If we do not value our ability to observe and make choices, we end up just reacting and wanting to blame the other person. This kind of response fits the archetype of a child or a victim. "S/he started it!" From a young age, we are taught that two wrongs don't make a right. Yet even as adults, it is tempting to want to point fingers. It seems our ability to observe can be so clear when we are looking at the other person. There is such a tendency to want to "remote control" others. The more we avoid observing ourselves, the more ineffectual we become at creating what we want. The more our "scanners" are pointed toward others, the less clear our own guidance becomes.

One of our greatest acts of power is to own the amazing ability we have to observe. Owning this ability as adults gives us the power to figure out, moment to moment, choice by choice, what a truly loving relationship looks like, feels like, and acts like.

When working with clients who were tortured at a young age and as a result developed multiple personalities, I was struck with their amazing ability to still have one personality that knew what was going on with all the other personalities. There is some intrinsic ability I believe we all have to not lose our "observing self."

There was a comforting but also deeply sobering YouTube video that a young man named Brad put on the Internet describing in very few words, which he held up, his three experiences with dying. He explained that he had a very serious heart condition. He wrote about seeing a bright light and experiencing such peace and then being brought back. He talked about observing the people who were trying to resuscitate him. He said that he felt such peace that he did not want to leave that place. At the age of eighteen on Christmas Day, 2011 he died. That was his final dying experience, and he did not return. In his willingness to describe his previous dying experiences, he taught us about our observing self. His observing self could see him unconscious with people working to resuscitate him. He was aware of his thoughts and feelings even as his body seemed to be completely unconscious and dying.

How much more can we benefit from this aspect of self during our everyday living experience? This observing aspect of self gives us an ability to truly see and be aware. With this awareness, we have the power and response ability to choose what we create.

Homework: Learn to utilize our ability to observe.

1. We are not just a bundle of impulses, thoughts, and feelings. We need to observe what is going on in all the various aspects of self. For example, "I just sounded defensive. Why am I responding this way?"
2. Practice observing your inspiration, thoughts, feelings, and body. Notice what is driving your responses and experiences. Is it love or fear? Choose the loving response.

Summary

We all have a built-in "observing self" as an aspect of our guidance system. This observing self has the ability to constantly monitor all information the spiritual, mental, emotional, and physical aspects of self are communicating. If we are honest, this information lets us know whether or not we are getting closer to or farther from creating and sustaining a truly loving relationship. Listening and responding to this inherent guidance is the foundation upon which we can build and create true love.

PART THREE

Creating True Love

Mastery Lesson:

We must understand and constructively respond to our core needs in order to create true love.

CHAPTER ELEVEN

Core Needs

We have been discussing the various aspects of ourselves and how each aspect is giving us important guidance so that we may choose to discover a truly loving relationship. The good news is that, even though we are receiving what may seem like volumes of information, it all comes down to something very simple.

Our "observing self" knows that all of this information is perpetually telling us whether or not we are getting closer or farther away from fulfilling our core needs for love and connection and safety and adequacy. Whether we are aware of these needs or not, these core needs drive everything that we think, feel, say, do or don't think, feel, say, or do. (I use the words love and connection because I think both words together provide a fuller meaning of this core need. Just as safety and adequacy captures more completely the essence of this core need.)

Moment-by-moment, the desire to fulfill these core needs can be driven by the power of fear or love. Choices made to fulfill these needs based on utilizing the power of our love ability allow us to continue to create and sustain a truly loving relationship with

NANCY L. DAVIS, LMSW, LMFT

ourselves and others. Choices to get these core needs met driven by the power of fear ultimately lead to disempowerment and disconnection.

Everything that is being communicated to us spiritually, mentally, emotionally, and physically, our observing aspect translates into what needs to **stop or start** so that our core needs are met. Any attitude, thought, or action that disempowers us or others needs to **stop**. The misuse of power ultimately results in increasing discomfort, pain, anguish, anger, bitterness, resentment, divorce, etc. Attitudes, thoughts, and actions, which utilize the power of our love ability, need to **start** and continue. These choices allow our core needs for love and connection as well as safety and adequacy to be continually met.

To state it differently, when we utilize our response ability (or power) to choose what creates loving connection, we also fulfill our need to know that we are safe and adequate. If we are responding from a place of fear, a truly loving relationship cannot be created or sustained. Responses grounded in fear seek to disempower and control others as a way to feel safe and adequate. Some of these strategies include insulting, minimizing, interrupting, dominating, comparing and contrasting, rationalizing, denial, blaming, shaming, intimidation, manipulation, projection, etc.

If our response perpetuates fear or disconnection as a way to feel adequate, we will ultimately destroy love as well as adequacy. It is like the game we played as children when we would be blindfolded and someone would say, "You are getting colder" (or hotter) until we arrived at the right place. Within each of us is a constant feedback loop guiding us toward the fulfillment of these core needs. We, however, have the power to ignore, rationalize, and continually override this guidance.

This may seem simplistic, but I am once again reminded of the analogy of the computer. It is my understanding that all the amazing complexity of the computer at the very core of its functioning is distilled down to ones and zeros, which literally communicate whether or not electrical energy is flowing (on) or not flowing (off).

The challenge is, while these core needs are driving everyone, we may or may not be consciously aware of what they are. Without this understanding, we are controlled by habits and historical patterns, which can easily lead us to having too high of a tolerance for what needs to stop in our lives and not enough tolerance for what needs to start.

Even though there is something painful occurring that needs to stop, if it feels normal to be yelled at, insulted, shamed, or to feel stupid, like a victim, unattractive, unlovable, etc., we can continue tolerating these experiences. Until finally some or all aspects of self make it clear, with increasing pain and discomfort, that we can no longer tolerate what has been going on.

My clients in recovery call it hitting a "bottom." When we finally hit that bottom and somehow find the clarity to know that something has to change/stop, it is the beginning of lowering our tolerance for what we believe is normal. Step-by-step, choice-by-choice, we start to increase our tolerance for creating and experiencing what is truly loving and safe.

If we were to make a list of everything that seems important, for example, work, relationships, children, sex, a pet, sunshine, food, fun, exercise, makeup, respect, a home, not having mosquitoes in the house, etc., everything on our list would reflect our desire to get one or both of these core needs met. We could also make a list of things that we may or may not want to own are important to us. For example, drinking too much, yelling, pornography, eating too much, lying, gossiping, spending too much, arguing, etc. All of these activities or attitudes are also reflections of wanting to get one or both of these core needs met.

For example, exercise could be an important expression of how we love and connect with ourselves by choosing to stay healthy. It could also be a way of meeting the need for safety and adequacy by feeling strong and powerful. Yelling is another example, according to many of my clients, of trying to be heard, which reflects the need for connection. The loudness of yelling can also reflect the need to be powerful and therefore adequate.

In general, while we are all being driven to fulfill these core needs, our responses may be coming from a place of fear and scarcity ("I'm afraid I won't be heard unless I yell.") or from a place of love and abundance ("I feel so much better when I take care of myself."). Yes, because of our habits and history, we could actually be trying to get our core need for love and connection met by being extremely unloving. Just as we could also be responding to our core need for safety and adequacy by making choices that lead to us feeling even less safe and adequate. I will describe this more in the next few chapters.

Even though we all have the same core needs, we all have a tendency to focus more on fulfilling either our need for love and connection or our need for safety and adequacy. Historically, there was a gender expectation that women would be the ones who cared about love and connection in the family and men would take care of the safety and adequacy needs by going off to work and providing for the family. We know that this paradigm of expectation often led to women feeling dependent, vulnerable, trapped, and closer emotionally to their female friends than their spouses. It also led to men feeling like they had to always appear strong and fulfill their function of providing without ever considering other needs they may have had. As these compartments have come down, it has become more obvious that both genders need to experience love and connection and safety and adequacy.

Still, today I have noticed that most couples, even same-gender couples, seem to be comprised of one person that leans more toward love and connection while the other leans toward safety and adequacy being the most important core need. This difference can either lead to both people becoming more whole, aware, and appreciative of each other as they each learn to become more balanced and complete or to a power struggle about which core need is really important.

Jane and Kathy both had careers and both wanted to have a family. In time, both birthed a child. While they both enjoyed being with the children, they decided that Kathy would be the stay at home parent while the children were young. They decided this because Kathy seemed to be the one who really enjoyed making a home and nurturing the children. While Jane very much loved the children, she really enjoyed going off to work and providing for the family.

Within about a year, Kathy discovered that she was actually jealous of Jane having the opportunity to go to work and be with other adults during the day. She missed bringing home a paycheck. She did not like the feeling of having to ask for money. She felt that Jane did not value all that she did around the house. She also wanted Jane to help take care of the children when she returned from work. Kathy was afraid to speak up about her feelings because she was afraid that Jane would get angry. It seemed safer to stay quiet than it did to tell Jane how she was feeling.

After some encouragement, Kathy did start to talk about her feelings with Jane. Jane, however, felt confused. Wasn't Kathy the one who wanted to stay at home? Jane was also not feeling appreciated for what she was doing to provide for the family and felt somewhat jealous that Kathy got to take the kids to the gym and go to a yoga class. She felt like she worked all day only to come home to Kathy expecting her to work all night with the children. She also felt that when she tried to help out with the kids or around the house, she was criticized. This left her feeling angry, inadequate, and like she could not do anything right. She had given up trying to help because she thought Kathy liked doing everything her way.

Growing up, after her parents divorced when she was six, Kathy was left alone after school with her younger siblings while her mother was working. This left her with the feeling of being overwhelmed, abandoned, and responsible at a very young age. Because she was a very capable child, eventually taking care of the younger kids became a way for her to feel special and powerful. If she did receive any attention from her mother, it was usually because of how well she was taking care of the house and children.

Because at some level it seemed normal for Kathy to feel overwhelmed, abandoned, and responsible, it was extremely difficult for Kathy to speak up, sooner rather than latter, about the things that were bothering her. By the time she did, she had lost the clarity of what she was feeling, why she was feeling that way, and what needed to be done. Instead, she just noticed generally feeling anxious and afraid of being rejected by Jane. She felt like she could not tolerate feeling disconnected from Jane when they had a discussion which did not go well. Kathy would end up feeling abandoned, and Jane would end up feeling angry because she could not do anything right.

Jane was raised with a father who expressed very little emotion and who wanted to avoid conflict at any cost. Her mother was labile, unpredictable, and hospitalized twice for severe anxiety. Jane felt like her father did not at all care about how she felt. He just wanted her to not upset her mother. She remembers feeling blamed for how her mother was feeling, as if she was responsible for her mother's severe anxiety. Jane got very good at repressing her own feelings. Her focus became doing well in school as a way to get out of the house and as a way to feel like she could do something right.

With reassurance that she would not be abandoned, and with practice, Kathy was able to start expressing what she was feeling and needing sooner. This clarity helped Jane know how to respond in a more effective manner. This led to her feeling much more adequate and appreciated rather than angry. Jane also became aware that her knee-jerk reaction was to feel angry when she felt confused. With some support, she was able to recognize this feeling of confusion and began to ask questions rather than react with anger.

This is an example of how two people worked together to strengthen their love and connection as well as their needs for safety and adequacy. Without their willingness to become aware and make different choices, each would have experienced more of what each feared most. Kathy could have ultimately either created her own worse pain by abandoning the relationship or being abandoned. Jane ultimately could have felt like a failure and inadequate because either she could not please Kathy or because of the relationship ending.

Once we recognize the central importance of these needs and the power they hold, we can begin the active choosing process. We can be grateful for the feedback loop which is perpetually guiding us toward what thoughts, attitudes, and actions need to stop or start so that we can craft a truly loving relationship with ourselves and others.

Being aware of our core needs for love and connection as well as safety and adequacy, and choosing to utilize our love ability to empower rather than choosing the power of fear to disempower, ultimately determines whether or not we can discover, create, and sustain a truly loving relationship. An in-depth discussion on how our core needs affect all of our relationships is next.

CHAPTER TWELVE

Love and Connection

Love and connection is an innate need that we all have. As a graduate student, I was shocked to read about the different levels of care young children were receiving in an orphanage. The research showed that the very young infants who were picked up and given attention lived, while the babies who were just changed and fed had a much higher death rate. Such basic care and connection made all the differences as to whether or not a child survived.

We all can remember throughout our lives how much happier we felt when we were given positive attention, when we felt loveable, and when we felt connected with a group that cared about us. Maybe because these needs are so intrinsic, we seem to never consciously stop to consider, "How am I creating love and connection in my life?" What seems to be more common is that we notice when someone else is not being loving. We then have a tendency to be unloving back by being judgmental and the cycle of feeling unloved and disconnected continues.

In general, if we are making choices which bring us closer to experiencing love and connection, we feel happier and more empowered to create our heart's desires. If we are getting farther away, we feel less lovable, less capable, and more fearful. All our aspects of self are constantly giving us our GPS instructions. When we listen and respond, we will be guided to a truly loving relationship with ourselves and others. It is much like the process of flying. It is my understanding that flying is a constant process of course correction until the destination is reached. It is never a perfectly straight line that can be followed. We are the same way. Through feeling discomfort, we know that something needs attention. Discomfort is an indicator that something unloving and disconnecting is going on. How we respond to this discomfort is an extremely important decision.

In flying, the choices are fairly straightforward. It is necessary to go up, down, left, or right in order to correct the flight pattern so that the destination can be reached. In life, we must determine the source of discomfort using the information received spiritually, mentally, emotionally, or physically. Once again, the choices are fairly limited. Is the discomfort coming from my attitudes, thoughts, and/or actions or from someone else's attitudes, words, and/or actions? Once the source is identified, there are only two directions to head in. There is either something that needs to **stop** and/or there is something that needs to **start** in order to reestablish a loving experience.

Whether we are conscious or not, we are all constantly constructively or destructively correcting our course in order to get our core needs met. The needs are constant. How we respond varies greatly. Ironically, out of fear and ignorance, we can try to get this core need for love and connection met by being very unloving.

Destructive unloving choices to meet our core need for love and connection are driven by the history and habits of fear and past wounds. Because so many of us have not grown up in a truly loving home, we really don't know what loving ourselves or others really sounds like, looks like, or feels like. But because this is such a core need, we are unconsciously always looking for ways to get this need met. Here are some of the destructive choices that can be made.

Destructive Choices to Create Love and Connection

The first example of a destructive choice to meet our need for love and connection occurs when we become dependent on others to get these needs met. We are consciously or unconsciously hoping someone will come along to meet this need. We need someone to prove to us that we are in fact lovable. This leaves us vulnerable to suicidal thoughts as adolescents or even adults when someone says they love us but they leave us instead. A deep sense of desperation can occur. It can feel as if we are not going to survive. We may fear that our need to know that we are worthy of love and connection will never be met again, and we feel like dying.

Wendy and Amy had been together since they were in their midtwenties. Amy thought they were very happy together. She had never felt loved by her parents who were cold and aloof. She felt that Wendy's love had healed such a deep sadness inside of her. They had purchased a home, enjoyed traveling, created successful careers, and had a lot of fun with their shared friends. One evening when Amy walked in on Wendy kissing one of their friends, in a split second all that she valued most was destroyed. Everything she believed about love was devastated. Her sense of self was deeply shaken and she became suicidal. She had never known such pain. Her joy, hope, and well-being had become dependent on what she thought was true about her relationship with Wendy. When that was shattered, she was shattered.

In time, Amy came to understand that Wendy was deeply wounded also. The truth finally came out that Wendy had actually had several affairs during the time she was with Amy. Amy had idealized their love. She had not understood Wendy's need to keep proving her own lovability by having other people interested in her.

In time, through therapy and contemplation, Amy was able to understand her child-like version of love and began to see the impact of her own wounds as well as Wendy's. She was able to own her lovability. She was no longer dependent on someone to prove that to her. With that awareness, she was able to be more honest and to see the "good, bad, and ugly" in herself and others. In time, Amy was able to choose a relationship in which she and her new partner were both willing to do the work of healing past wounds as well as the work to cherish their love and connection. Even though her trust and innocence and hopes and dreams were shattered, Amy came to be extremely grateful that she had lived long enough to experience the incredible joy of true love.

A second destructive choice occurs when we are willing to be manipulative just to keep someone from leaving. We may not care about what is best for them. We just don't want to be left alone. Some mothers are infamous for using guilt as a way to manipulate their children in order to keep some kind of connection with them. This also occurs in couples when someone says hurtful, undermining statements as a way to make someone feel unworthy of anyone else ever loving them.

A third destructive choice occurs when we allow others to manipulate us. Rather than using our mental, emotional, or physical discomfort to guide us away from someone who is unloving, we push the guidance away and become defensive so that we can hold on to what is unloving.

Women who have been battered mentally, emotionally, and/or physically are vulnerable to wanting to stay with their abusing spouse. The need for connection, even without love, is so strong some women have been killed because of it.

Sandy came from a verbally and physically abusive family and married someone who also abused her. For so long, she believed all the insults and threats. She did not believe she was loveable. One day out of desperation, she took a shotgun and drove away, believing that death was her only escape from the physical abuse. Luckily, a neighbor who knew about the abuse saw Sandy leave with a shotgun and called the police. Miraculously, they were able to find her and take her to a safe house. Sandy eventually found the strength to press charges and leave the state. After getting an education and working in therapy to strengthen her love ability, Sandy was able to create a very different loving empowering relationship with herself and her partner.

A fourth destructive choice occurs whenever we are so focused on the other person that we lose our ability to speak up or act on what we know to be true. When we busy ourselves with our spouses/partners, and what is going on with them, we allow ourselves to rationalize, enable, and/or behave in a codependent manner. When this occurs, we become unable to notice or speak up about how our relationship could be more loving and therefore deepen our connection. In silence, we allow resentment to build, creating a growing disconnection, rather than face our discomfort and fear of speaking up.

Mary and Ned had been together for many years. For many of those years Mary had just tried to please Ned as a way to get her needs met. She did not feel powerful and would often not speak directly about what she wanted or what was important to her. As time went by, she became more judgmental and resentful toward Ned because he was not very good at meeting her unspoken needs.

Her judgment was subtle, but over the years, Ned felt unloved and inadequate to please Mary. When this was pointed out in therapy, Mary was almost shocked to realize that he was feeling the same way she was. She also felt unloved and inadequate. She came to realize that she had focused so much on him that she had not adequately been letting him know what would have felt loving and connecting for her. It was almost as though she expected him to figure it out, even though she had never been clear about her wants and needs.

As Mary examined why she had felt inadequate to speak up, she realized that while growing up, no one asked or listened to anything she had to say. She learned that the only way she thought she might get any love was by taking care of her sick mother. In time, through therapy and reading about codependency, Mary recognized why it felt scary for her to speak up. She had to face inner feelings of shame and fear of rejection.

Through couples counseling, Ned understood more of what was going on with Mary and he was able to encourage her to speak up. He was relieved to realize that it was not helpful for him to continue to try to read her mind. He also realized that he needed to speak up and participate in discussing what kind of relationship he wanted rather than just relying on Mary to make everything happen. Through this new process, it became clearer how he could connect with Mary in meaningful, fun, sexy ways, and he began to feel more adequate. Mary let go of being judgmental and began to feel grateful for the loving gestures Ned made toward her, which resulted in both of them feeling more loved.

This relationship is a good example of how fear and ignorance, even with good intentions, can ultimately lead to destructive choices which cause disconnection rather than a truly loving connection.

In contrast to these destructive strategies, the following describes what it looks like and feels like when we are responding to these core needs with the power of our love ability.

Constructive Choices to Create Love and Connection

The first way we know that we are responding to our need for love and connection in a truly loving manner is when one plus one becomes more than two. Each of us knows that our life is better because of the loving relationship we are creating and nurturing every day by the choices that are made. We each know that we are worthy and that our inspiration, thoughts, feelings, and physical well-being matter. By valuing what each of us brings into the relationship, we are thriving more fully together than if were separate.

Amy had worked on healing her past as a child of an alcoholic. She had worked hard to accept that she was loveable. She had become a strong, articulate woman that others looked up to. Kevin was also in recovery from an addiction to alcohol and had been sober and working his program for many years. They met through the recovery community. Both had previous relationships which did not last. Together they chose to come to therapy to learn how to consciously create the relationship they desired.

They knew that through learning and applying the recovery steps, they had a chance to experience life very differently. Because of that experience, they both had the openness and humbleness to want to learn and practice how to maintain love and connection. Together, they learned how to create the joy of coming home where they felt cherished, where laughter came easily, where struggles were quickly resolved, and where they each had the freedom to create shared and separate endeavors.

They both realized what their past wounds were and they each took responsibility for them. If they lapsed into seeing things through the lens of past wounds, the other person knew what was happening and did not take it personally. At the same time, they each had the expectation that they would continue to talk things through, go to meetings, and go to therapy when needed. Because of these choices, they both remained very grateful for their relationship, and they both knew that their lives were better off in every way because of each other.

A second constructive choice to create true love and connection occurs when each individual owns his or her response ability and utilizes it to make loving empowering choices. Choosing to create a truly loving relationship can inspire us to be the best we can be. With the intention to honestly take responsibility for our choices, it becomes increasingly clear whether or not we are thinking, saying, and/or doing what creates a truly loving connection.

Everything we think, feel, say, or do is either strengthening or disempowering to our relationships. Negativity, judgment, blaming, and disdain are draining and straining and cause us to feel depressed, tired, anxious, withdrawn, ill, and unhappy. Choosing positive loving thoughts, attitudes, and actions renews our connection perpetually to that which is empowering and allows us to feel hopeful, creative, clear, peaceful, inspired, and happy.

Whatever we focus on grows. We know that no one is perfect. There is always something in life that we could feel discouraged or encouraged about. Every thought, attitude, or action we choose is creating our reality. Brick-by-brick, thought-by-thought, word-by-word, action-by-action, we can utilize our response ability to create love and connection.

A third constructive choice to sustain love and connection occurs when we utilize our ability to speak up, if disconnection has occurred. When we lovingly speak up about what is said or done, or not said or done, which feels hurtful, we can then reestablish a loving connection as soon as possible. This is a very positive process of course correction.

It is normal to have feelings occur which are uncomfortable. These feelings can surprise the person that triggered them because it was not at all their intention to make these feelings happen. This is an opportunity to discuss the feelings as well as an opportunity to appreciate what was intended. With this awareness and willingness to talk about the feelings and the good intentions, disconnection can quickly turn into an even stronger connection. The choice to listen to the guidance of our discomfort allows our relationship to continue to move forward, deepening our love.

The process of speaking up sooner rather than later is like the difference between missing one exit when you are traveling so that you can quickly get back on track versus noticing that somehow you ended up in a state that you were not planning on visiting. It is better for everyone to find out sooner rather than later if disconnection has occurred.

A fourth constructive choice to create love and connection occurs when we differentiate the present relationship from

past relationships. No matter what has happened to us in the past, if we choose to consciously use our present connection to create a truly loving relationship, amazing healing can occur at every level. In order to accomplish this, we must be here now. By actively choosing to be in the creative present rather than recycling the past stories, which will never change, we can differentiate and create who we want to be today. This also allows us to appreciate and see who our spouse or partner is striving to be today. We can only be alive in the present. The past is gone and the future is not here yet. Living in either of these dimensions robs us of the loving connections that are only possible in the here and now. As others have said, that is why it is called "the present."

Summary

Many of us are vulnerable to clinging to connection, even when it is not a loving connection, as long as we believe, at some level, that a destructive connection is our only hope to experience love. The truth is each of us has the potential to generate a loving relationship starting with ourselves. I am not referring to a narcissistic relationship where it is "all about me!" Choosing to create a truly loving relationship, starting with ourselves, means that we have the potential to discover and own not only our own lovability but also our "love ability." From discovering the abundant source of love that exists within, we will notice our love ability as well.

So often you hear people say, "You can't love someone else until you love yourself." I know the good news is that we don't have to wait until we perfectly love ourselves before we can start utilizing our love ability. In this process of loving ourselves and others, it is necessary to be balanced. We need to be able to listen and respond to what it means to love ourselves as well as someone else. The importance of maintaining this clarity and balance allows us to stop moving toward narcissism, codependency, passive-aggressive behavior, or any other destructive expression of connection based in fear and past wounds, rather than true love.

What is true is that the more we own our lovability and treat ourselves and others lovingly, which means with compassion, patience, kindness, self-control, and generosity, the more our love ability is empowered. There is a reason that one of the most basic spiritual messages in all the great religions is, "Love your neighbor as you love yourself." To live that truth would transform all of our relationships. Each of us has this transformative potential living within us. One moment, one choice at a time, we can listen to our guidance and choose to respond in love.

Homework

1. Honestly describe how you have either destructively or constructively been trying to create love and connection in your life.
2. With each of the constructive choices or ways to create love and connection which I have listed, **ask yourself, "How am I, or could I, create this experience in my life?"** For example, with the strategy of knowing that one plus one is more than two. First, consider how your life is better off because of the relationship you are in. Second, ask your spouse how his or her life is better because of you. If you are not better off because of your present relationship, describe what would need to change in order for this to become true.
3. Continue this process with each of the constructive strategies. "How am I, or could I, honestly take

responsibility for my choices to create loving attitudes and actions toward myself and my spouse? How am I, or could I, constructively speak up when disconnection occurs? How am I, or could I, choose to live more fully in the present?"

CHAPTER THIRTEEN

Safety and Adequacy

We have been discussing the first set of primary needs, which are love and connection. The second set is safety and adequacy. These needs again are so innate that most of us don't stop to think about how they drive our responses. We all want to feel safe spiritually, mentally, emotionally, and physically. We want to feel adequate to create the life we desire. When we do not feel safe and adequate, we may respond by feeling anxious, angry, or other uncomfortable feelings. Even if we do not really understand what triggered those feelings, our guidance system gets activated, and if we are listening to our feelings, we know something is wrong.

While growing up, if we did not feel loved, we also may not have felt safe. It is also true that if we did not feel safe in some way, we may also not have felt loved. These core needs of love and connection and safety and adequacy, go hand in hand.

As children, we seem to have trust and innocence and assume that our parents love us and want us to feel safe. Unfortunately, with experience and time, if these needs are not met, we learn to defend ourselves in some way. Our defenses can be denial, repression, storytelling, anger, stealing, addiction, etc. until one day we leave home. Unconsciously or consciously, we would like to leave those experiences behind. Many of us seek to create committed relationships as a way to feel loved and safe, only to discover that we have created life as we used to know it rather than life as we still wish it could be.

Work is another place where we hope to at least feel adequate. Maybe we have special training or have advanced degrees. However, depending on who we work with or for, we may or may not feel safe and adequate there as well.

Ultimately, whether or not we are able to get our needs for safety and adequacy met, is determined by how we use our power. A discussion about safety and adequacy is really a discussion about our power and how we utilize it. Many women I work with get uncomfortable with the word *power* because so often physical or mental power has been misused against them. Disowning the power we have does not make us any less powerful. It just means that we are not **consciously** using the power we have. This usually results in our power coming out in some indirect, passive, manipulative manner.

Our power is like our breath. It is always present, abundantly emanating from us in every thought, attitude, or action. If we make the choice to constructively use our power to empower ourselves and others, we will create safe and adequate relationships. Constructive use of power always empowers and benefits each person in the relationship. It creates win-win situations where each can thrive and no one is diminished. Decision by decision, we come to trust our ability to create. Others come to trust, respect, and feel safe with us as well. This is the kind of relationship where love and connection flourishes as well.

The destructive use of power occurs when we are engaging in power struggles. Power struggles are driven by a sense of scarcity and fear. There is a conscious or unconscious belief that there has to be a winner and a loser. Someone has to be right and someone has to be wrong. Power struggles are an attempt to lessen the other person. This desire is based on a distorted belief, that, if someone else is less than, "that must make me better than." This, however, is not true.

Every time we argue, debate, attack, attempt to dominate, and/ or "be right," we are also becoming "less than." We become less than able to see/hear the other person accurately in terms of their love ability, legitimate concerns, potential to create goodness, etc. Unfortunately, we also become less able to fathom our own love ability, power to create abundantly, inner wisdom, etc. Whenever projection, denial, and judgment are utilized, we are diminished. We may not even recognize the cost and the consequences. In fact, we may actively defend against this awareness by rationalizing the power struggle: "I was just trying to be clear." "But I was right." "If he (she) would just listen, I would not have to yell."

Temporary ego gratification never permanently leads to true safety and adequacy. No one wants to feel like they are being controlled or that they are less than, so the power struggles continue. In time, power struggles erode any love and connection that may have existed. Power struggles are never pretty, and they are definitely never sexy.

This destructive use of power results in relationships where spouses barely speak to each other (or are constantly bickering) and have not slept together in years and/or divorce. When parents misuse their power, it may result in grown children moving as far away as possible. Power struggles at work between managers and workers or between coworkers result in people feeling like bitter, angry, victims or leaving in search of a better work environment.

Once again, our creative course correction comes down to what needs to stop or start. Let's start with learning more about some of the specific destructive power struggle strategies which are driven by fear and result in us actually sabotaging our ability to be safe and adequate or sustain true love.

Destructive Choices to Create Safety and Adequacy

The first example of a destructive power struggle is "the great debate." This power struggle seems to be driven by the belief that whoever is "right" is the adequate one and whoever is "wrong" is the loser. The fight goes back and forth, usually with many interruptions and talking over each other, until someone can't take it anymore and is verbally and mentally beaten down.

While there may be a momentary feeling of victory, anyone who has engaged in such battles sooner or later learns that, love, happiness, safety, etc. are not won by making someone feel "wrong" and "winning" the debate. This point is ultimately driven home when love and sexual intimacy no longer exists and divorce follows.

This strategy has confused being "right" with being adequate. There is actually very little in the complexity of relationships, which can be reduced to "right and wrong" and yet many arguments are fueled by this desire to be "right." One of my favorite bumper stickers reads, "Do you want to be right or do you want to have a relationship?"

There have been many couples who have come into therapy wanting me to be the referee and tell them who is right and who is wrong.

After working with Jean and Gary for a little while, one day Jean stated that she had not realized how her behavior had contributed to their relationship not working well. She actually felt relieved and empowered to learn about what she could do to create a very different relationship. With a smile on her face, she confessed to me, "At the beginning of therapy, I thought we would come in here and you would tell him all the things he was doing wrong."

My experience is that most people intend to have a successful loving relationship. However, most of us also want to be right as a way to feel adequate. Because of the often unconscious fear of what it would mean if we were wrong, we end up focusing on what we think the other person should be doing. Consequently, because we cannot control the other person, we end up feeling frustrated, angry, hurt, and inadequate to fix the relationship.

A second destructive choice to misuse power is the "parallel tracks" discussion. This often occurs when one person is talking about how they are **feeling** while the other person is on a parallel track, defending their **intensions.** These separate tracks never connect, and both people end up feeling unheard and uncared about because neither person is willing to change tracks and care about what the other person is feeling or intending. **One of the most fundamental determinates of a couple being able to heal and thrive is whether or not each person is willing to trust the good intensions of the other.**

Once a person is willing to accept that their significant other was not really intending for them to be hurt or feel whatever it was they were feeling that was so upsetting, we can now talk about what the feelings are about.

The parallel tracks process can be a very volatile source of conflict between people because intentions speak to the essences of the person. On many occasions, I have heard one spouse say to the other, "If you don't know me better than that, what hope do we have?" Without intentions being acknowledged, we can feel irrelevant, inadequate, and worthless. We can feel the devastating effects of past traumas and wounds being projected onto us. This can feel intolerable for most people.

On the other hand, feelings can feel so intense and real that it is difficult see or hear anything beyond them. However, the **beliefs or stories we are telling ourselves** about the other person's intentions are so often what fuels the intensity of feelings.

As a couples therapist, I have often interrupted a very emotional process to ask, "Was it really your intention for her/him to feel . . . ?" So often, the feeling can much more easily begin to shift and heal when the real intentions are acknowledged. Finding a way to hear and acknowledge both the feelings and intentions brings us back to the same track of working on the relationship together.

Jackie and Pete had been in couples therapy long enough to at least take my word for the importance of acknowledging each other's intentions and feelings. When Jackie started to talk about Pete, she would preface it with, "I know it wasn't his intention, but . . ." Jackie was very intelligent. At first when she started saying this phrase, it felt like she had been listening to me but was not really convinced that it mattered what his intention was.

In time, I saw and felt the relief in Jackie's face and tone as she was able to separate out what she had been projecting onto Pete. She had compassion for herself and what she had gone through as a child. However, she could now acknowledge that he really loved her and trusted that he did not have the intention to make her feel inadequate. This was coupled with her more actively speaking up and taking care of herself as well. By Jackie choosing to utilize her power constructively, she no longer needed to see Pete as ineffectual in caring for her. She could see his strengths and weaknesses and appreciate how he expressed his love for her.

The third destructive use of power is the claim of being "psychic." Fairly frequently when couples are discussing something, I have heard one of them say, "I know what she/he *reeeeeally* meant by that!" Especially with couples who have been together for a long time, there is often an air of self-righteousness when this pronouncement is made. They then proceed to talk for the other person and tell me what she/he was really thinking or feeling. Even though we may believe we know more about the other person's thoughts and feeling than they do, it does not necessarily make it so.

Many times, I have slowed the discussion down and encouraged couples to actually hear each other. I then follow up with the question, "Do you believe what they just expressed?" There is often a pause because of the internal conflict between letting go of their "psychic" belief or story about the person, which they have become quite attached to, versus hearing the truth of what the other person is **actually** thinking or feeling.

A fourth destructive use of power is the "defense attorney" stance. This process occurs when someone is attached to a particular case against their spouse or partner. They defend their version of reality by beginning their sentence by using "You" liberally, bringing in examples of past behavior (the witnesses), as well as quoting what other people think or have said about the person (the experts). In closing, some kind of pronouncement usually ends their presentation.

As you can imagine, this way of trying to feel adequate by arguing against someone else's adequacy does not end well. This is particularly destructive when someone is genuinely making an effort to create positive change (which no one can do perfectly overnight) and as soon as old behavior occurs, the defense attorney jumps all over them to "prove" their case that nothing is really different.

A fifth destructive use of power as a way to feel safe is the "freeze out." Shutting down verbally, withdrawing affection or attention, withholding sex, etc., as ways to induce guilt and punish the other person, sabotages love and connection and is a destructive use of power. I know many women and some men have resorted to these strategies because they feel so overwhelmed and ineffectual. The passive use of power is an extremely effective way to destroy any possibility of creating true love.

In some relationships, individuals do not feel safe or adequate to create what they desire. They believe that if they did speak up, it would not make any difference. Intentionally disconnecting, as a way to try to manipulate some outcome, will never lead to true love. All that remains is either going through the motions of a meaningless relationship or further disconnection until divorce occurs.

A sixth destructive use of power is the "bullying" strategy. Any form of attacking the other person as a way to feel powerful is tragic at best and illegal at worst. Verbally shaming, blaming, insulting, and/or threatening, destroys any hope of ever having a safe or loving relationship.

Physically hurting anyone is illegal and should never be tolerated. Any form of abuse is usually tolerated in a relationship, when a person has been mistreated as children. Having high tolerance for abusive behavior is a very serious symptom of being wounded and is potentially dangerous. It is very important to leave and/or seek help immediately, if this is the kind of relationship that is being experienced.

These are just some of the primary ways I have witnessed many people misusing their power with their spouse or partner. When any of these strategies are occurring, it erodes the connection between people until the love is gone and all that is let is an ongoing power struggle.

Now let's discuss some of the constructive choices which are empowering rather than disempowering. These choices all lead to a deep sense of safety and adequacy and with that, a sense of confidence that a truly loving relationship is possible.

Constructive Choices to Create Safety and Adequacy

The first example of constructive use of power is the choice to effectively listen to ourselves and others. The difference between our ears just hearing and actually effectively listening is that we are listening for accurate meaning. Using our power to listen to what is being expressed and why leads us to a meaningful response. Meaningful responses lead to effectively creating what we want rather than what we don't want. Ongoing effective listening gives the guidance necessary to connect our desire with our outcome. We all desire a successful relationship. Effective listening gives us the power to actually create one.

Wanda and Henry often lapsed into interrupting each other. It was clear from listening to this process that each would only partially hear what was being communicated before launching into a response. When Harry was first asked to try effective listening, it was clearly difficult. It felt like he just wanted to hurry up and parrot what was being said so that he could go ahead and say what he would have said anyway.

With practice, something more peaceful began to occur. They were each working to understand what the other person had actually said and meant before responding. They discovered that they enjoyed this experience much more than their interruptive verbal battles. Clearly, this process allowed them to begin to more effectively create the kind of relationship they desired.

A second powerful choice to meet our need for safety and adequacy is to create work that is enjoyable and meaningful. It is important that we value what we *do*. Once we become adults, we are no longer children or victims; we are responsible. Having "response ability" is an amazing opportunity and gift to be free to create. Finding a vocation or avocation that is expressive of our potential is one of the most joyous things we can do for ourselves. Most of us are full of creative power and potential, and without a constructive focus, we stagnate like a cesspool.

Our energy is meant to flow and be directed toward something constructive where we can thrive, not just survive. When we empower ourselves and utilize our response ability to take ownership of what we do for work, this positive energy flows into our relationships as well. Without making this choice, too often our time to be with our spouse or partner is spent complaining about work rather than building a loving connection.

Frank and Lucy both worked all day. When they got together for dinner, all too often their conversation was about work. This left them both feeling frustrated and inadequate. Either they felt like their situation was not really being understood or they felt like the other person was trying to tell them what to do. It also seemed to escalate the level of anxiety or agitation that they both continued to feel throughout the rest of the evening.

After accepting the homework assignment to stop talking about work and start talking about what they would enjoy doing together that evening or on the weekend, they both reported how amazingly better they felt. When work did come up, they began to focus more on what they actually enjoyed about work or what they were choosing to do to create change at work.

Using their response ability at home to create more of what was enjoyable empowered them to appreciate and create more of what they wanted to experience at work as well.

A third constructive choice to rightly use our power to create safety and adequacy is to discern when to say no. Being able to say no and not just yes is a huge positive act of power. Sometimes, with very young children who are just beginning to experience their power, we can hear them responding to whatever is said to them by saying, "No!" This, however, is not what I am suggesting.

Being able to say no and not just yes means that we have to pause and determine truly what we think and feel before responding. That pause is a crossroad between finding our own voice and just rubber-stamping what someone else is saying. Finding the truth of our own thoughts, feelings, and inspiration in a discussion determines whether or not someone is being diminished or two people are honestly getting to know each other.

Historically, women have been especially vulnerable to "people pleasing" as a way to be liked. Unfortunately, without being honest with ourselves and others, there is always that nagging question of, "Do they really like/love me?"

I have pointed out to many clients the importance of being honest from the beginning of dating. We really are better off knowing, sooner rather than later, whether or not there is enough compatibility to sustain a connection. Unfortunately, if we put the cart before the horse and attach to a relationship before we really know each other, the outcome will not be what we desire. In time, the truth always comes out. It is always better to build a relationship on what is true. Truth/trust is the foundation upon which love can grow. Without this, we will never feel safe or adequate in our relationships, and love will not thrive.

We must be able to claim the legitimacy of having limits or our life force will be drained out of us. We are not meant to be human sacrifices. We must know where we begin and end. We must be able to have a sense of boundaries and know what is or is not our responsibility, what is or is not comfortable, desirous, interesting, sexy, etc. Without this distinguishing awareness of self, we cannot directly take care of ourselves. We either become vulnerable to being controlled by others or vulnerable to wanting to control others. This way of wanting to control others is an indirect manipulative way of trying to be powerful through someone else and never works well.

Zoey and Stan seemed to be a very loving couple, but they had a tendency to not speak up when something was bothering them. This eventually led to both of them feeling bitter, angry, and/or resentful. During our couple's session, I would frequently hear (almost like a punctuation mark) at the end of someone's comment, "I did not know that. She/he did not tell me this."

As they each did the work to recover from being codependent, they began to be more aware of their own feelings, thoughts, and needs. They were, therefore, much more able to discuss their concerns and differences, even before they arrived for their therapy session. Facing their fears about what the other person might think liberated them to create a relationship which truly reflected their needs and wishes. I could see in their faces and hear in their voices how much happier they were in their relationship.

A fourth constructive choice to utilize our power is to face any fear or wounds we have been avoiding or defending against. Finding the courage to notice that everything that we have a tendency to be judgmental about is a reflection of something within us that we want to disown can be the beginning of a liberating journey to joy, love, and accomplishment.

Whatever we disown owns us. It limits our view of others, ourselves, and what we are truly capable of creating. When we stop projecting onto others what we want to disown, when we stop attacking others as a way to defend against our vulnerability, and when we start facing what we need to focus our response ability on in order to heal, only then can we more fully know the healing potential which exists within us. Only then can we adequately empower ourselves to discover, create, and sustain truly loving relationships.

A fifth constructive choice to utilize our power is to choose to be open to loving ourselves and others. Love is an active, powerful choice and it has a natural tendency to follow the fourth choice we were just discussing. When we turn and lovingly face ourselves with compassion and forgiveness, being open no longer feels dangerous. Rather, it feels truly liberating and empowering.

Openness gives us the inspiration and the clear vision we need to determine what needs to be healed. As we face our wounds and use our power to heal, we no longer need to engage in power struggles as a way to feel adequate.

Here is an example of a couple who found a way to overcome many of the power struggles which can be encountered in relationships. Rather than staying stuck and focused on defending their wounds, they found a way to face their fears and empower themselves to choose the love they both desired. Betty and Mike had been together for several years. Betty was an attractive woman who had struggled with being overweight. Even though Mike regularly reassured her of her attractiveness and of his interest in her sexually, she constantly watched Mike to make sure he was not looking at other women. This, of course, was an impossible expectation of Mike, because there were always other women around.

While Betty clearly wanted love and connection, even though Mike was offering it, it was not valued. She continued to question her lovability and his ability to love her. Mike never got to feel adequate at expressing his love. This also resulted in him not feeling loved by her. After a date, rather than enjoying sexual intimacy, they would argue about who he was or was not looking at.

While Betty wanted to be loved, because she did not feel loveable, she set up an impossible standard for Mike to meet in order to prove to her that she was loved. This resulted in Mike feeling inadequate, angry, and insignificant. He also did not feel safe to be honest. Of course he noticed other women, but he loved and was attracted to her. With Betty withholding sex, because she did not feel attractive, he turned to the Internet for sexual activity, which he knew would also be used against him—if she knew.

Betty and Mike had not mastered the second lesson we have discussed, which is to know who we are so that we can create what we want, rather than what we do not want.

The emotional aspect of Betty was not being listened to. Betty was not asking herself, "What am I feeling and why am I feeling this way? What do I need to do about what I am feeling?" Without asking herself these questions, she could not access the answers, which were, "I am feeling afraid and unsafe. I am feeling that way because of the sexual abuse I experienced as a child." Without facing her past wounds, Betty was continuing to feel unsafe with Mike and could not figure out what to do about her feelings.

Betty thought she wanted love and connection, but because of her abuse, unconsciously it was even more important for her to feel safe by being in control. Therefore, she was going to argue, debate, shame, criticize, and do whatever it took to defend against feeling vulnerable and unsafe again, which is how she felt when someone was attracted to her. Even if it took proving to herself that the man that loved her did not really love her.

Once Betty was able to face her fear of sexual attention, she was able to begin her healing journey. Betty was able to stop projecting her fear onto Mike as if he was someone to fear. She was able to start looking at the many ways she had been misusing her power against him and herself. She faced that she had been misusing her body to gain weight in order to keep men away. She started to own that she really did want to be loved. Betty also began to see that she had been rejecting Mike's love as a way to feel powerful and safe. By recognizing that she had actually created a relationship where she could be safe and loved, in time, Betty was able to begin to have more realistic expectations of Mike. This allowed their date night to turn into a time of deepening their connection rather than using their time together to have power struggles about who was right or wrong.

Mike had to realize that he was feeling inadequate and that trying to please her by meeting unrealistic expectations was a setup for failure. He recognized he had questioned his "adequacy" and had been trying to prove his worthiness to Betty. Instead of trying to prove that he was not noticing other women, he began to tell the truth. He did notice other women, but he wanted to be with her. He found the courage to speak up and acknowledge that food was being misused in their relationship. Mike was able to discuss his feelings about the weight they had both gained. He realized he did not want to continue misusing food as a way to be close to her. Betty acknowledged that through Mike having the courage to speak honestly, she actually was feeling safer with him. Because they both made the choice to face their fears, they both felt safer in their relationship and they both acknowledged feeling even more in love with each other.

Summary

We all want and need to know that we are safe and adequate. Unfortunately, without actively considering how we are using our power, the tendency to create power struggles will actually undermine our ability to be safe and adequate. Power struggles are based in fear, ignorance, and scarcity. As long as we are trying to be safe and adequate at the expense of someone else, love and connection will never survive or thrive.

Using our power to effectively listen for meaning, to create meaningful work, to say no in order to create appropriate limits and boundaries, to liberate ourselves by facing our wounds, and finally to choose to be open to a truly loving relationship are some of the most "power full" choices we can make. Finding the courage to respond to our core needs for safety and adequacy by making these choices will ensure that true love can thrive.

Homework

1. Honestly describe what kind of power struggles you have initiated or gotten hooked into responding to. Remember how you felt afterward. Remember the impact that it had on your relationship.

2. Look at each of the constructive choices to utilize your power. Honestly determine what steps you need to take to utilize your power in order to create a safer and more adequate relationship. For example, with the first choice to do effective listening to determine meaning, you might ask your spouse to discuss something with you so you could practice how to become better at this process. (See steps on how to do effective listening, which is included in the "Truly Loving Practices" chapter in this book.)

3. Continue this process with each of the choices to constructively empower yourself or your spouse. For example, if you are not enjoying your work, take time to determine what is or is not working for you and what might be done. What are the steps that would need to be taken?

Where do you appropriately set limits and say no, and where do you still need to be honest and speak up about your likes and dislikes?

What are your vulnerabilities and wounds? How are you owning and addressing them? If this is unclear, it can be helpful to ask someone you trust to help you identify how your past wounds are still being acted out today.

Finally, how are you actively being open to loving yourself or others? How are you allowing others to love you?

PART FOUR

Sustaining True Love

Master Lesson:

We must make loving choices to sustain true love.

CHAPTER FOURTEEN

Truly Loving Practices

True love is discovered, created, and sustained by making truly loving choices. It is an ever evolving, deepening experience based on each attitude, thought, and action we choose. We are perpetually destroying or creating love and connection and safety and adequacy. The accumulative truth of our choices is reflected in the degree to which we are experiencing true love.

If we are willing to listen effectively to the communication we receive from our various aspects (spiritual, emotional, mental, physical, and observing self) and accept the meaning of our guidance, we will know what we need to stop or start thinking, saying, and/or doing. By feeling the sadness, anger, pain, strain, etc. of disconnection and power struggles or by feeling the warmth, joy, peace, etc. of love/connection and adequacy/safety, we will always know if we are utilizing our love ability and response ability to make constructive or destructive choices. As the Chinese proverb states, **"To know and to not do, is to not yet know."**

Now that we know more about the guidance we receive from our various aspects and the core needs that drive us, let's consider some of the most basic choices we must practice or do in order for true love to thrive. These practices bring *knowing* and *doing* together and empower us to create and sustain truly loving relationships.

The Practice of Effective Listening

Usually this has been called "active" listening, which implies that it is not a passive process. I agree that effective listening is an active process. From working with very capable people, I have learned that there is a big difference between active listening and effective listening.

Being able to actively repeat what the other person has said, until the other person acknowledges being heard, is just the first step. Effective listening is also about rightly using our power to maintain and deepen our love and connection with each other. **Being willing to not just hear the words but also the meaning allows us to more effectively resolve any misunderstanding we may have.** Effective listening leads to communication, which strengthens the connection between people. It is never about who is right or wrong.

There will always be misunderstandings in relationships because we are not clones of each other. But misunderstandings or conflicts are never what destroy a relationship. It is what we do with our different experiences or perspectives that will determine if true love will thrive.

If we are attached to defending our version of reality because we only feel safe and adequate if we are "right," we will destroy the possibility of deepening and strengthening our love. I often compare conflicts or misunderstandings to a car wreck that two people are describing. Our descriptions will never be the same. It does not mean that one is right and one is wrong. Through effective communication, both people will feel heard and understood. Our view of reality will expand, creating healing opportunities, and love will flourish.

Homework: Learn effective listening.

Step one: First person expresses himself or herself with no more than three sentences.

Step two: Second person repeats what the first person said.

Step three: First person acknowledges that the second person heard accurately. If it was not heard accurately, it is repeated again. (This is like trying to make sure you heard the directions clearly. It does not make sense to move on if you are going in the wrong direction.) We return to steps two and three until the first person has been accurately heard.

Step four: Second person interprets the meaning of what the first person said and **asks if that is the correct meaning**. (It is very important that a question be asked as to the accurate meaning. This is not a chance to make a pronouncement about what the other person meant by what they said.)

Step five: First person acknowledges that the meaning was correct or clarifies what the meaning was.

Step six: Only now should the second person express what his or her thoughts and feelings are. Again, the response should be only in three sentences or less before pausing to repeat the above process.

NANCY L. DAVIS, LMSW, LMFT

Only with accurately understanding the meaning of what the first person said does it make any sense for the second person to share thoughts and feelings. Without this process in place, we are vulnerable to taking off in all kinds of reactionary directions, which sabotage our ability to create love and connection. Effective communication gets easier with practice. It is a necessary skill which we must master in order to create and maintain a truly loving relationship.

The Practice of Owning Our Story

We must all appreciate the experiences which have shaped our strengths and vulnerabilities. There are infinite ways that our core needs have or have not been responded to while growing up. We cannot know why similar circumstances leave one person prone to being desperate for love and someone else desperate for a sense of safety. But what we can do is notice our own core vulnerability. Understanding and owning our story is the beginning of being able to love and connect with ourselves. It is the beginning of owning and legitimizing that we have power and that we can use it to create what is true love.

If we have disowned our wounds through denial, projection, minimization, dissociation, etc., we have stuffed them away in what I call our "belief box." All of our earlier experiences crystallize into beliefs about everything and everyone. These beliefs are not necessarily true, but they completely determine how we see ourselves and others. Even if we do not know what is stored away in this belief box, these beliefs still own us and control our actions and reactions. Disowning inevitably leads to projecting our story onto everything and everyone. This occurs because we need our external reality to match the reality we have stored in our belief box.

Just like the story I shared about Betty and Mike, consciously she thought she wanted love and connection, but the deeper wound demanded that she react, even to a loving relationship, as if she were not loved so that she could feel safe, even if she had to project a hurtful story onto the one who loved her most.

Knowing our story and facing it can liberate us from the unconscious power it has over our beliefs about ourselves and others. This is not something that has to take years of analysis to figure out. Every day we are who we are. All of our wounds at a core level leave us feeling not loveable and/or not safe/adequate. Once we recognize our core wound and the stories that we continue to project around that wound, it is possible every day to observe how our thoughts, feelings, and actions continue to make that wound a reality today.

We have the ability to "crank back our blinders" and notice what is actually true or possible today. By making the choice to stop projecting our past onto our present, we can then start to think, feel, and act differently. Each truly healing thought or action gradually transforms our experience, allowing us to clean out our old belief box and replace it with a consciously created new chapter of life.

Sally was raised by a mother who one minute would say, "I love you" and the next moment may draw her close and say, "I hate you!" This kind of erratic behavior left her chronically feeling anxious. As she matured, she came to believe that no one was really safe. It was only a matter of time until they would lash out. When she and her spouse came to me, it was clear that their relationship was in trouble. Karen felt that she was irrelevant. It did not seem to matter what she really thought or felt or intended; Sally would make very negative pronouncements about Karen's motives and meanings.

After Sally brought in a recording of thirty-two hostile messages her mother had left on her answering machine, it became clear that she had been raised by a mother who had a borderline personality disorder. With this understanding, Sally was able to begin to read about this disorder and understand what her experience had been growing up. She realized that her partner was definitely not her mother and she began to stop projecting negative expectations onto Karen. This understanding led her to being able to embrace the love that they shared.

Being able to understand her developmental story was ultimately liberating. She was able to start to see herself and other people very differently. Not only did her relationship with Karen begin to thrive, but her relationships with people at work also became much more comfortable, as she no longer expected the worst to happen.

Homework

Write your developmental story. Describe what is in your "belief box" about yourself, love, others, safety, power, trust, and sex. Identify how past experiences have most influenced your core needs for love and connection and/or safety and adequacy. Consider how others and you have used power to either empower or disempower. Write a new chapter that describes the kind of relationship you want to create with yourself and your spouse/partner.

The Practice of Realistic Expectations

We all have expectations of ourselves and others. They may or may not be clear, stated, or conscious, but we quickly have the opportunity to discover what they are every time we are hurt, angry, irritated, disappointed, etc. Most uncomfortable feelings occur because something is going on that we did not expect.

Unfortunately, when these uncomfortable feelings occur, most of us react by focusing on the person that we think should fulfill our spoken or unspoken expectation rather than pondering, "What was I expecting and was it a realistic expectation?"

By focusing on the other person, usually you will get one of three possible reactions. One reaction is, "I'm so sorry. How can I fix the situation?" (If someone's core wound is questioning their lovability or worthiness, they are often willing to take responsibility for something they did not even know was expected of them.)

The second very common reaction is, "What are you talking about?" (If someone's core wound is questioning their adequacy, they are often quick to become defensive if a situation makes them feel that they have done something "wrong.")

A final choice might be, when an unknown expectation has occurred, to say, "I'm confused. I did not know you were expecting this from me." This would be the most aware, and therefore the most helpful, response.

Most people would be most comfortable with someone else taking responsibility for their unknown or unspoken expectations. This is inevitably a setup for failure for both individuals involved. It postpones the possibility of being able to consciously create what we desire. Rather, it sets into motion a normative process where mind reading is the expectation. If that process continues, the relationship will become like a house of cards, and collapse is the inevitable future.

It is inevitable that we will all have unspoken expectations as long as we do not know what is stored in our belief box. Unspoken and unknown expectations inevitably come from our disowned core wounds. We bring them into all relationships. However, the pain, anger, and disappointment are most deeply felt in our most intimate relationships.

It is as though we unknowingly bring our dowry of wounds into our committed relationships and hand them over to the other person to heal. Because we all have wounds and both individuals are unconsciously handing their wounds over to be healed, most relationships cannot withstand the hurt and disappointment which are the result of these unrealistic expectations.

We unknowingly want and expect our spouse/significant other to be able to heal our wounds. This of course is never stated or consciously spelled out as an expectation. Instead, we just react with judgment and self-righteous indignation when an unspoken or unknown expectation is violated. Often we state or imply that the need was obvious, therefore ensuring that the other person will either feel inadequate or fight back and defend his or her adequacy. This process obviously destroys love and connection.

We must be willing to do our homework and ask ourselves, "What am I feeling, why am I feeling that way, and what do I need to do about that?" Without effectively listening to ourselves, we will never be able to determine realistic expectations of someone else. If we truly want to give and receive love, our expectations of ourselves and others will be doable. There will not be an unconscious setup to prove to yourself or others that love and safety are never possible. No one will need a crystal ball in order for us to feel loved and for them to feel adequate.

I have often told my clients that life is on a continuum. On one side is what we can control and on the other is what we cannot control. Unfortunately, because of what many of us have experienced growing up, it is not always clear what goes where on the continuum. We either want to control someone or something which we cannot control or we want someone else, who loves us, to have such power. Consequently, we end up with unrealistic expectations of ourselves or others.

With a willingness to learn from the discomfort that results from unrealistic expectations, we can learn to deeply value what we can do rather than what we cannot. In this acceptance, true love can thrive.

Betty and Bill had been together for twenty years. Betty was experiencing severe anxiety and was unhappy in their relationship. Bill cared very deeply for Betty but did not really know what to do to make her happy. When I asked Betty what she thought would make her happy, she said, "I really enjoy dancing." I turned to Bill and asked if he was willing to go dancing with Betty. Bill said, "Yes, if that is something she would enjoy."

As a young therapist at the time, I thought, *This is very hopeful.* However, very quickly, Betty responded, "But I want him to want to!" Willingness to go dancing out of love for Betty was not enough for her to be happy. She expected his feelings to be the same as hers for his gesture of love to have any meaning to her. This expectation sabotaged her ability to take in his love.

I have often had male clients who have stated that they wished their wives wanted to have sex as often as they did. Others have wished that their wives would initiate having sex. While discussing this with one couple, I asked the wife how often she would like to have sex. She replied, "He initiates sex every day. I have no idea how often I might want to have sex. There is never enough time between sexual encounters to figure that out." She was not complaining

NANCY L. DAVIS, LMSW, LMFT

and she was willing to have sex frequently. However, his wish for her to initiate sex was not allowing her to feel adequate in their relationship. His focus on her initiating sex also did not allow him to fully appreciate the love she had for him.

I have had to clarify with many husbands the reality of the influence of testosterone. Most women will never have the same biological urge to have sex as frequently as most men because they will never have the same levels of testosterone. While taking into account the biological differences, it is important to openly discuss and decide how physical connection will be strengthened and maintained.

Unrealistic expectations will only undermine the ability to value the "half-full" part of the glass. To truly love ourselves and others, we must consciously decide to have realistic expectations. The practice of determining what is or is not realistic to expect allows us to release expectations, which result in pain and disappointment. This frees us up to focus on appreciating and enjoying what each person realistically can bring to the relationship.

Homework

1. Name one thing that you feel disappointed about in your relationship. Disappointment is usually the "feeling clue" which will help us understand what we have not fully made conscious. For example, some people never really had a chance to play when they were young and long for this experience. If parents did not model this as okay behavior, it is easy to be left with the desire but not the "permission" to make it happen. This need can result in an unspoken expectation, which can come out as, "You never want to have fun."

2. Take ownership of this disappointment and talk about this with your spouse by only using "I" messages. For example, "I would really like to go dancing. I was wondering if you would be willing to go dancing next Saturday." This process allows us to take ownership of our wounds and empowers us to do something about them. This can transform our relationship into a truly loving, empowering experience.

3. Make a list of experiences you would like to create. Pick one and decide the first action step you will take this week.

4. Once that first step is taken, notice how empowering it feels. Now decide what the next step is and when you will take that step.

The Practice of Forgiveness

The practice of forgiveness is built upon the practice of effective communication, owning our story, and making a choice to have realistic expectations. Without these previous practices, we will never get to forgiveness. We will be caught up in a cycle of rationalizations, which will fuel shaming and blaming someone else for our pain and discontentment. Inevitably, love and connection are strained until love is lost and only our pain, grievances, and power struggles remain.

The practice of forgiveness adds to our ability to create what we really want. Forgiveness is about release. We release ourselves from the destructive force of focusing on misunderstandings because of ineffectual communication. We release ourselves from projecting our past wounds onto our present relationship. We release ourselves and others from the setup for failure because of unspoken or unrealistic expectations. As we release all of these processes which

NANCY L. DAVIS, LMSW, LMFT

are hurtful to ourselves and others, we become available to choose the practices which are healing and helpful. Practicing forgiveness is liberating and joyous. It frees us to see ourselves more clearly and experience more deeply the joy which comes with accepting that in our imperfection we can choose love and compassion.

Forgiveness is not our initial human reaction when we feel hurt, misunderstood, neglected, abandoned, betrayed, violated, or any other kind of pain. Without thought or consideration, our knee-jerk reaction is to attack actively or passively or both. This is what we see countries, celebrities, politicians, athletes, etc. doing to others every day in the media. Unfortunately, but not surprisingly, in our most intimate relationships we all too easily do the same thing when any kind of misunderstanding occurs. Our best hope of being able to create true love in relationship to ourselves and others is to make the choice to practice forgiveness. While it may not seem to be easy, I guarantee living a life where love thrives is much easier than the alternative.

Linda and Harry had only been dating for a short period of time when they happened to run into someone that Harry used to date. After a brief conversation, they continued on their walk. Almost immediately, Harry sensed that something had changed in Linda's mood. At first, he attempted to ignore it, but finally Linda said, "Do you still have feelings for her?" Harry was actually shocked by the question because he was enjoying their relationship so much more. As Harry stammered out an answer, Linda continued with, "I really don't want to be abandoned again."

This experience let Harry know that Linda not only projected her past onto him but she had also chosen to abandon the wonderful connection they were having that afternoon because of the story she had started to tell herself.

After some time to think about the experience, he was able to bring the incident back up to discuss with her. He expressed his concern about feeling irrelevant because he already had been through that kind of relationship. He knew his own story and he was not interested in recreating it with someone else. She immediately recognized what he was talking about. She apologized and realized that she definitely did not want to continue to do this to their relationship. She decided to return to therapy to work on separating her past abandonment experiences from the present.

With open conversations and the willingness to forgive each other, if they slipped into projections from the past rather than remaining in the present, Harry and Linda were able to strengthen and deepen their love. They were able to set their relationship onto a sustainable course, by utilizing the practices I have been describing, and have now been together for many years.

Forgiveness is a choice. It is a choice to see ourselves and others more honestly. When we look into the mirror of relationships, what do we see? Do we see our own imperfect humanness staring back at us? If so, choosing to forgive will come more easily. Compassion, peace, and love will follow.

However, if we choose to stay unconscious and project our wounds onto others, we will rationalize, judge, blame, shame, argue, intimidate, along with any other defense necessary to keep ourselves from recognizing ourselves in that mirror. If we were all perfect robots, love would have no meaning. When we humbly accept and work toward healing our own wounds and imperfections, laughter, love, and forgiveness come more easily.

Homework

1. Forgive yourself for the many ways you have been judgmental toward yourself and others. That may sound like, "I forgive/release myself and my spouse/ partner from all judgments. I recognize holding onto grievances has kept me from fully loving myself and my partner/spouse. I release all the stories and rationalizations which have hindered our love from thriving. **Today is a new day in which I choose to focus on and do thriving, loving, empowering, practices.**"

2. Choose to be aware of any resentments, judgments, or disappointments toward yourself or others, which need to be recognized, learned from, and then released through forgiveness. This awareness comes from practicing, "What am I feeling? Why am I feeling this way? And what, if anything, do I need to do about this?" Be thankful for the guidance of being uncomfortable. Don't throw the gift of awareness away like a hot potato, projecting it onto someone else.

The Practice of Talk Time

For most people, life seems to be very busy. Just trying to get the daily to-do list done seems to be a perpetual practice in feeling ineffectual. It seems there is always more that could've, should've, but didn't get done. The treadmill of busyness never stops on its own. As I reminded a friend of mine recently who was describing the craziness of her week, "Don't forget who is in charge."

When there are children at home, the to-do taskmaster seems even more in charge for some people. Making time to talk seems like a luxury, and yet it is a necessity to stay connected and clear about how to create what is desired. If couples and families do not decide on a "talk time," it is replaced by the "yell out information from separate rooms or on the way out of the house" time. This usually leads to either a "talk at you" or "yell at each other" time. Obviously, the practice of effectual listening does not work well from separate rooms.

Talk time is the time to pause and consider, "How are we doing? How are other things going? What would we like to create and experience together?" People are constantly changing. This is the time to make sure we continue to grow together rather than apart. Talk time, in navigating and creating thriving relationships, is equivalent to checking the map to make sure we are on course. Talk time is the foundation upon which sexy time is built. Without having a way to maintain our loving connection spiritually, mentally, and emotionally, the physical connection will not thrive.

Here are some guidelines to creating an effective, balanced, meaningful talk time.

1. Set aside a consistent time, day, as well as the amount of time to be spent each week, with additional times being added if needed. I recommend starting with thirty minutes.
2. Clarify at the beginning what each person would like to discuss. Having a clear agenda helps us stay focused on what really matters.
3. Make sure that the time is shared by each person. If one person is not participating in talk time, it becomes a "talking at" time. Sometimes one person will say, "I don't have anything to talk about." First of all, that is not usually true. Second, it is code for many things,

such as "I have not taken the time to consider what I need to talk about" or "I expect you will do all the talking anyway so why bother?" Recognize when disconnection is beginning and make a different choice. Keep talk time balanced so that everyone is participating in sustaining connection.

Homework

1. Decide and schedule when and how long your talk time will be.
2. Set your agenda, share the time, and always reschedule your next talk time so you know when it will be.
3. After you are successful as a couple creating meaningful talk time, consider creating family talk time to include the children as well.

The Practice of Date Night

Date night is an essential practice for relationships to thrive. Once again, this practice is built on all the preceding thriving practices. The purpose of date night is to remember why you like and love each other. Dating, initially, was how you got to know and ultimately love each other. This is the experience that led to you both wanting to live the rest of your life together. Obviously, there is something very important about the experiences that took place while you were dating.

I can honestly say that I have never met a couple who said that they loved to do laundry, go grocery shopping, have every date night at the same restaurant, watch movies the other person did not enjoy, complain about work, or forget about their date during the time they were dating. Yet, while working with couples who have been together for some time, I have heard all of these examples as date-night experiences.

Date night is meant to wake us up, make us notice, and remind us of the joy of living life together. It is a chance to renew our energy by having fun, creating new experiences, celebrating successes, dreaming together about all kinds of things, and strengthening the physical bond by engaging in sexual intimacy. It is time out from all the to-do lists. It is an essential time to be together. This is where the foundation of a relationship continues to grow stronger and deeper. This is a time where we come together to nurture, deepen, and perpetually renew love. Falling in love ten years ago is not what keeps a relationship thriving. It is being in love today that is meaningful. To perpetually be in love today, we must continue making loving choices for love to thrive. Date night is one of those essential choices.

Without sexual intimacy, most relationships will not last. This level of intimacy differentiates our primary relationship from all other relationships. Without this physical intimacy, our relationships become like ticking time bombs. It is only a matter of time until they either explode or implode. In all my years of working with couples, I have frequently said, "If I care more about your sex life than you do, you're in trouble." Not having sex becomes one of those disconnects that so often both people want to ignore. As a therapist, I know it is like the big elephant in the middle of the room. It is only a matter of time until it cannot be ignored.

The energy that comes from loving sexual intimacy can renew us physically, mentally, emotionally, and spiritually as well. We are whole beings. Connecting fully allows true love to thrive.

Homework

1. Take turns creating a date night, remembering this is a chance to have enjoyable experiences together.
2. Choose a block of time when you have the energy to have fun experiences, including sexual intimacy.

The Practice of Gratitude

Gratitude is the truly loving practice of seeing ourselves and others clearly and choosing to cherish the strengths we see. When we have chosen to effectively communicate so that we actually hear each other, when we know and take response ability for our own wounds and can therefore have realistic expectations of others, when we choose to love and rightly use our power to build a life together through the release of forgiveness, when we perpetually grow and have fun together through talk time and date time, the expression of gratitude perpetuates all that we want to strengthen and grow. It does not happen if we are taking each other for granted. It does not happen if we are focusing on the half-empty part of the glass. Gratitude creates a quick renewal of joyous connection. We invite the warmth of a smile when we see clearly and choose to express our appreciation.

Gratitude is a choice. For too many of us, it seems so easy to notice what could have been better, what is missing, or what we wish could be. Unfortunately, because whatever we focus on grows, if we choose a negative focus, we will frequently miss out on what is wonderful and what we are glad is there. Without the practice of gratitude, relationships deteriorate to maintaining the function of daily living, which may or may not be enough to keep a couple together. Making the choice to practice gratitude allows us to value who we are and who we are with. The practice of gratitude is one of the most powerful ways to create and sustain the joy of a truly safe, loving relationship.

Maybe you also saw the picture of the mother, sitting in a lawn chair in the front of her home while holding a sign that read "On Strike." When interviewed, she listed all that she had been doing for so many years for her children and her husband. She did not feel appreciated and she was done.

Unfortunately, this happens all too often when couples take each other for granted. I remember a comedian who talked about her relationship. She said that it meant a lot to her to hear that she was loved. When she pressed her partner about this he said, "I told you once that I love you. If anything changes, I'll let you know."

Knowing that you are appreciated for mowing the lawn, doing the laundry, picking up the kids, being successful at work, bringing each other water so someone doesn't have to get up, looking handsome, smelling good, being patient during that time of the month, shoveling the snow, sharing kind words, being affectionate, being sexy, or making the bed—there obviously is an infinite list— matters.

Choosing to notice what we are grateful for is choosing to see someone with loving eyes. Gratitude is one of the most powerful antidotes for judgment and projection. We are perpetually observing each other consciously or unconsciously. Every negative judgment is like swallowing a drop of poison. At first, it goes unnoticed, but in time, it costs us our ability to create what we all seem to desire, which is a truly loving relationship. Expressing gratitude in our relationship strengthens our ability to see all the talents and gifts that we have taken for granted while we were focusing on the half-empty part of the glass.

Homework

1. Make a list of all the things you appreciate about yourself.
2. Make a list of all the things you appreciate about the other person.
3. Keep that list and express gratitude about at least one of these things every day.

CHAPTER FIFTEEN

Continuing the Journey

Many people begin the journey of healing their relationship with the sense that they are climbing a steep mountain and feel the force of gravity pressing down upon them. At the beginning, people often express how difficult it seems to change and go against gravity. I reassure them that the journey is never perfect and sometimes it will feel like they are taking three steps forward and one step back, but I have seen what is possible, am familiar with the journey, and with the willingness to learn and do their homework, healing is possible.

After listening to their struggles and concerns, I begin their education by drawing four circles on top of each other and four more across from the previous four. I then describe that each circle represents the primary aspects of who we all are. I then write "Spiritual," "Mental," "Emotional," or "Physical" next to one of the circles. I then draw lines of connection or disconnection between the circles as a way of illustrating what they just described to me. I then explain that our relationships are like a piece of cloth. When disconnection occurs in these various ways, we feel very uncomfortable. We feel happiest when we feel connected and safe, not when the relationship is starting to fray and pull apart. I then name the feelings that were being expressed to me of pain, anger, anxiety, blame, sadness, etc. as forms of communication. Each of these feelings has been telling them that something is very wrong. Through pondering the meaning of what they are each feeling and why, we will then figure out what needs to stop or start in order for the pain to subside. At this point, I usually see nodding heads. This understanding brings more hope and willingness to take the next step along their healing journey. Then I give them their first homework assignment.

For those of us who have taken this journey and have made it up the mountain one step at a time, we know that it was the most important and most challenging journey we have ever taken. I guarantee no one who has made it up the mountain of change wants to return to his or her old life. The view, the joy, the fun, the peace, the meaning, the experience of discovering, creating, and sustaining true love is nothing less than transformative. Many people laugh with acknowledgment and relief when remembering how they used to live and feel when we first met.

We are complex beings truly beyond our full comprehension. We are receiving an abundance of guidance from our spiritual, mental, emotional, and physical aspects, which our observing self (when listened to) can translate into what needs to stop or start in order to create a truly loving relationship with ourselves and others. If we are honest with ourselves, love is like the light from the lighthouse shining through our fog, guiding us to shore. We all want to go where it will lead us.

We are driven by our needs for love and connection as well as safety and adequacy. If we do not consciously listen and constructively respond to these needs, we will unconsciously, destructively respond to these core needs. These destructive choices delude us into thinking we are doing something necessary. However, inevitably these destructive choices lead to the loss of love and the futility of power struggles.

Understanding and choosing to apply truly loving practices liberates us from the delusion of projection, fear, and judgment and frees us to discover, create, and sustain the joy of true love toward ourselves and others. "To know and to do" empowers us to clear away the clouds of pain and confusion by stopping what needs to stop. Knowing and doing empowers us to listen and respond to what needs to start. One step at a time, one choice at a time, our journey leads us farther up the mountain until one day we are no longer controlled by the pull of gravity. Until one day we notice that the view is simply divine and the knowing laughter of true love is shared.

It is my deepest hope that each reader has begun his or her transformative journey and that this book will continue to act as a helpful guide. By now, the power and importance of focusing on what we want to create are hopefully very clear.

Here are closing thoughts to begin or end each day with.

May true love be my guide.

May I release all thoughts of fear and scarcity and replace them with thoughts of love and abundance.

May I release all power struggles and replace them with peace.

May I release all guilt and grievances and replace them with compassion and forgiveness.

May I continue to discover, create, and sustain true love.

ABOUT THE AUTHOR

Nancy L. Davis, LMSW and LMFT, has been a practicing psychotherapist for thirty-five years. She has been in private practice for the last twenty-five years. Her specialty has been working with women and couples. During her professional career, she has taught at various seminars and conferences as well as at the University of Michigan.

For the last several years, her volunteer work has focused on being on the Great Lakes Regional Executive Board for the American Friends Service Committee for three years, being the chair of the Michigan Inclusive Justice Program for one year, and singing in a choir.

Nancy was born in Michigan and was a long-time resident until she and her partner recently transitioned to living full-time in Coral Springs, Florida, where they enjoy biking and kayaking.

Nancy can be contacted at nldbooks@yahoo.com.

CPSIA information can be obtained at www.ICGtesting.com
Printed in the USA
LVOW06s0049150913

352447LV00001B/2/P